LIKE A *Butterfly* WITH SORE FEET

Like a *Butterfly* With Sore Feet

Struggling to Balance Marriage, Family and Ministry

Pastor Eric L. Jordan

XULON PRESS

Xulon Press
2301 Lucien Way #415
Maitland, FL 32751
407.339.4217
www.xulonpress.com

xulon
PRESS

Printed in the United States of America.

Paperback ISBN-13: 978-1-6312-9078-7

Ebook ISBN-13: 978-1-6312-9079-4

Dedication

This Book is dedicated to the most beautiful woman in the world, my wife Faith. I met her at a college dance on the Campus of the University of Texas. I was not a student there but was invited by my best friend Wayne and his girlfriend Natalie. It was arranged to meet them at the event called "Soul Night Dance" on a Saturday night. I drove down from Abilene Tx, more than three hours to get there. My cousin Fred drove down with me, but once we arrived, we couldn't find Wayne at the dance hall. After about thirty minutes, I call my buddy Wayne, "Dude, where are you?", he says, "Man, I'm not gonna be able to make it." I reply, "Dude, I just drove three and a half hours to to come down here; what do you mean you're not going to make it?" He says, "Man, I'm with my girl and we decided to stay at home." Well, though I was a little upset, I could get with that, they were in love! Fred and I sat on a bench outside the dance hall as I hung up the phone. Suddenly, two girls walk by and I am blown away by this beautiful angel as she struts by. Her friend seemed to disappear in her beauty, I barely noticed her friend after I saw this mysterious woman with a sexy walk and dimples I could see from across the hall. I think my heart literally stopped as she was walking by. I said to Fred, "Dude," that was the expression in the '80s, "Dude, look at those girls walking by!" He said, "Man, do you want me to call them over?" I said, "No let's catch-em on the dance floor." But Fred calls them over anyway. Then Fred says to the one with the light brown skin, perfect teeth, long hair and a body that just won't quit, "Hey, my cousin wants to know your name." Well, usually, I'm a pretty smooth operator, but Fred caught me off guard, and I replied rather awkwardly, "No, I don't.... but wait, as she begins to leave, "What's your name?" I was trying to be cool, and keep my "mack" on, if you don't know what "mack" is, it means, to be smooth, debonair and to pretend not to be interested, but I wasn't about to let this one leave without her name and number. She turned and said, "Faith." "Oh, my God, when she spoke with that soft voice and looked at me with her hazel-green eyes... People, if ever there were such a thing as love at first sight, that was it. I was done, I lost all my mack. As she walked away, I was speechless and forgot to get her number. I tried looking for her in the dance area for about an hour, but never saw her again. I told my cousin that night on the way back to Abilene, "If I ever marry anybody, it would be her." On the drive home that night all I could think about was this girl at the dance named Faith. The next day, I call my friend Wayne, "Ask Natalie, does she know a girl that goes to U.T. named Faith?" Now what are the odds, out of 40,000 students, she would know a girl named Faith, whose last name I could not remember? I hear Wayne ask her over the phone, "Do you know a girl at U.T name Faith?" Natalie says, "Faith Stone?" I yell over the phone, "Yeah, Faith Stone, that's it," she says, "Yes, I know her, we are friends." With a deep sigh of relief and overwhelming joy, I say, "Well, hook a brother up then!"

Faith and I have been married for over 30 years now with three gorgeous daughters, Brooke, Jade, and Layla, all of whom I am so proud of. God could not have chosen a more exceptional woman, wife, and mother for our children. Her inner beauty far exceeds her gorgeous smile and stunning appearance, if that is even possible. Faith, thank you, with all my heart.

TABLE OF CONTENTS

ACKNOWLEDGMENTS

With sincere and heartfelt warmth, though you can't see me, I'm applauding and giving a standing ovation to the best editor in the world: Tigist Helen Schmidt. You have been amazing and so encouraging in this process of writing my first book. All the suggestions and ideas have been helpful and made me feel at ease. It's as though you were divinely placed in my life for such a time as this.

To my brother Jerry Jordan, Big brother, you have been more instrumental in my life than you will ever know. Because of your acute discernment, I am preaching the word of God today. Furthermore, because you basically raised me, and led me to Christ, you accomplished the great commission; there is no higher duty than that.

To mother Ocelie Herring, who has now gone on to be with the Lord, but had the spirit of Anna a prophetess who did not depart from the temple but served God with fasting and prayers day and night. It's because of you, this book has been written because you persuaded me to write it.

Pastor Fred Moore, who encouraged me not to quit when the spirit of darkness tried to veil the light within me. Thank you, brother preacher.

Randal Marlin Casey, from the first time we met, you have been a supporter to me and my ministry. You are a man of God that wants the best for every believer, and I thank God for you.

My father and mother, thank you for bringing me into this world.

My surrogate mother and family, Rosemary, Earnest, Wendy, and Keith. Thank you so much for treating me as one of the family.

All my brothers and sisters, nephew, and nieces, who have supported me, I love you all.

To my church family, mainly elder Kevin and Yolanda White, who have stayed by my side through the ups and downs of ministry.

To my three daughters, Brooke, Jade, and Layla, without you, I would not know the meaning of life.

And best of all, my wife Faith, you are making me a better husband, father, and man. I never knew love really, until I understood, you are the love of my life.

To the late R.C. Sproul, I have been a partner of Tape of the month and Tabletalk Magazine since 2004. Your teaching exposed me to truths that changed the course of my theology. Though I only met you once briefly at a book signing, I feel through the years, you were my personal professor at our own private college. The title of this book is a reflection of what you once said on a CD. From afar, and never knowing my name, you have influenced me and the writing of this book.

And to my Lord and Savior Jesus Christ, who died for a wretch like me. No words can describe my gratitude, no number of tears can express my love and appreciation for the kindness you have shown me. You are my life, and without You, I can do nothing.

INTRODUCTION

So often we read motivational and encouraging books on how the author has had success in their life, whether it is a restored marriage, thriving ministry, flourishing business, miraculous healing, or overcoming insurmountable odds. But rarely are there books that focus on the arduous unpleasant journey without an apparently positive outcome. The market is full of self-help, positive thinking, and step by step books on how to change any circumstance in your life. I thank God for these encouraging stories and counseling that are available to us, but what about that in-between stage? The long determined trek it takes to reach the mountain top of a healthy marriage, the rocky road on the way to the blissful city of a harmonious relationship, the dark tunnel of despair approaching because of the loss of a child, or because you have been devalued and feel ignored in a relationship, or you no longer see hope because the forest with too many trees of regret and bad business decisions has caused self-doubt?

This is my life, fitted between happiness and misery. As a pastor, I certainly know how and where to find the answer for all of life's difficulties; but that does not exclude me from major trials and sometimes overwhelming tribulations, a struggling faith, and at times self- doubt. I know the victory is mine, but the battle can cause stress and anxiety until the victory comes. This is the focal point of the book: a regular guy who is not a big-time preacher or pastor with 3,000 members, nor do I have a perfect marriage or has had great success in business. I'm not a highly educated professional with a Ph.D., far from it. So why would my story be of any value to you? What nuggets of wisdom can you glean from my life? What could I offer that would somehow help you? The answer is because I'm just like you and we all have a story to tell that can help others through their battle and toil in life. I understand the frustrations you're going through because I have them too. However, wherever there is a problem, there is a solution. This book is both about the solution, but also, the exhausting expanse of time and human frailties between the problem and the solution. It is an honest and exposed personal look at a person dealing with a difficult marriage, a struggling ministry, business failures, tragic losses of loved ones, and coming to grips with his inadequacies, deficiencies, and sin.

My life is a life of testimony and trials, and a book that is not complete. I am still living out this journey while writing this book, but I pray as you go on this voyage with me it will bring some comfort to your situation, inspire you to stay steadfast amid chaos and disappointment and bring encouragement that you're not alone. In Christ, there is a balance that is needed to have peace of mind that God is bigger than any problem and will help us through every one of them.

What is **Balance?** ***Noun***–an even distribution of weight enabling someone or something to remain upright and steady. Synonyms: stability, equilibrium, steadiness, footing- "I tripped and lost my balance" 2. a condition in which different elements are equal or in the correct proportions. ***Verb***–keep or put (something) in a steady position so that it does not fall. -Oxford Dictionary

Chapter One

A Life Out of Balance

"The key to keeping your balance, is knowing when you have lost it."–Anonymous

[1]*"The mind is its own place, and can make a heaven of hell, a hell of heaven. -John Milton*

"I can't believe you treat me this way, it's always about you; you never listen to me and think you're always right. You always put your career before the family and me. Don't ever speak to me that way again! In fact, I'm not sure I can take this any longer, I just don't think it's worth it. I need time to think about our situation; I think we should separate for a while."

This is a place of despair, a life out of balance and a conversation every marriage will eventually have. It is a loud conversation I'm having with myself, and it's being replayed within my mind as I drive down a long country road in Texas. It is the fall of 2009, the last week of October, the weather could not be more perfect in central Texas. I remember it so vividly because, though it's a beautiful day with a bright warm sun and amazing blue skies, there's a stormy gray cloud encamped over my soul.

---

[1] John Milton, *Paradise Lost,* books IX and X notes, page 91, edited by A.W Verity, Cambridge at the University Press, 1962

On the outside, I pretend things are fine, but I know it's a lie. My life is at a fork in the road and I need a resolution. The mood is melancholic and I'm discouraged and frustrated about life, marriage, and ministry. Significant decisions and changes need to be made in my life or it will have a dreadful effect on me. My life is out of balance, and I don't know what to do; the scales have tipped in the wrong direction and I keep telling myself–don't do anything stupid. Has suicide entered my mind, never, but at this point in my life, I wouldn't mind if the Lord took me home to be with Him. It's a selfish thought but an honest one.

I'm on my way to a ranch near Coleman, Texas, in a beat-up white 2002 Ford Explorer praying it will make the three-hour trip. A friend, who owns the ranch has suggested I go there and spend some time alone, away from the hustle and bustle of a stressful time in my life. I met Randy when our church was in search of a new building to lease. We planted the church about a year-and-a-half earlier in a community building in downtown Round Rock, Texas. My wife Faith, and I, along with our three daughters, Brooke, Jade, and Layla, have lived in Round Rock since 1989. The church I pastor is about 35 members and growing, *slowly* The church decided to test the waters of moving to a location in a local neighborhood, nothing serious, just weighing our options. I called a realtor I found on the internet. I'm not sure why I chose this company but it seemed right at the time, he was the only realtor I called. Have you ever had a feeling, a compulsion, to do something and you don't know why?

The realtor met me at a place I had in mind, a small store-front type building about 800 square feet. It was something the church could afford. As I began to convey to the realtor, a very well-manicured impressive and humble young guy, he explained to me he had another client across the street that was about to list his building on the market. It was larger than what we had in mind. Right away I knew it was out of our range financially, but I also know my God says, "*Nothing is impossible- with Him.*" So, we head across the street, and with each second, my spirit is being stirred within me, there is a hope and a faith that rises, and my doubt turned to expectation.

We enter the building and the owner Randy comes from a room in the back; our realtor introduces us. After we looked at the building, we sat down to talk about the possibilities of leasing the space.

Immediately I sensed God moving; I began to explain to Randy how the Lord called me into ministry and what our vision was for God's kingdom. He was so moved he looked to his realtor and said, "I don't care what it takes, I want this man in this building." Wow! When you walk by faith and not by sight, God does move mountains. We leased the 2500 square foot building for the same price as the 800 square foot building.

It turns out Randy and the Realtor are Christians and wanted to see God's kingdom advanced. From that meeting, a special bond cultivated with Randy and me, and God has used him to be a blessing to our ministry for some time. The 300-acre ranch is where my story begins.

The Ranch

A Place of Serenity or not?

As I'm driving down the country road to the ranch, it's about 5:30 pm, and the sun is beginning to set. I have never been to this place before, and it's a little challenging to find. It is out in the middle of fields of cotton and rows of corn, filled with cows, horses, pigs, chickens, and tractors. I was born in Houston, Texas, a major city but raised in a small town called Abilene, that's right out of the cowboy books. I now live in the suburbs of Austin and it has become a metropolitan destination. I have never been on a ranch, or at least one this size. As I moved toward the ranch up a rocky road lined with cactus and tumbleweeds gently moving across it, I could see the quarters in the distance- a 5,000 square feet lodge on the hill. It looked relaxing and tranquil as the sunset bent down behind it, yet at the same time I have an unsettling feeling, it's as though all my senses are on high alert. As I carefully surveyed my surroundings while getting out of the Ford SUV, I noticed I couldn't see any other homes, anywhere. It seems I was indeed in the middle of nowhere.

As I walk toward the house the sun is setting and it's getting dark. I take a quick look around to secure my uneasiness. When I find the hidden key, I unlock the door and begin to grab my bags out of the vehicle. I walk toward the door with with luggage in hand, and my neck on a swivel looking for any wild animals that might want to eat me, or any critters that would slither or crawl up beside me. From the outside the ranch house is modest, but when I open the door, a gorgeous 30-bed home with a master bedroom, guest bedroom, full kitchen, living room, two pantries, four bathrooms, with a garage that holds 4 four wheeler motorbikes, a basketball goal, canoes, and kayaks; blows me away, and that's just the downstairs. As I made my way up a charming wooden staircase into the loft area made of polished redwood, there was a pool table, ping-pong table, games, TV, and more beds. I'm in this massive complex by myself, and I love it. I'm kind of a loner anyway; I think most pastors are; however, soon excitement turns into apprehension when I realize I'm a black man in the middle of nowhere in Texas at night, alone.

I know God did not give me the spirit of fear, but that scripture seemed to have slipped away, and thoughts of the movie "Deliverance," with Ed Beaty began to creep through my mind. You must see the film to understand what I'm referring to. At that moment I went to the kitchen to retrieve knives for each room and place them strategically where I knew I could find them if needed. I don't own a gun; although there were locked guns in the ranch house, however, the knives would do just fine. By nature I am a fighter and have been in plenty of fights growing up. So, in my mind, no hillbilly was going to make me squeal like a pig, as in that uncomfortable scene in the movie.

As I settle in and get ready for bed, one more check around the house, windows...check, doors...check, bathroom, and toilets... check, don't want any slithery critters hiding away in the toilet; which stories you hear about in Texas. After everything is secure I lay down in the quietest place I have ever been, and yet, I hear noises I have never heard before; after all, this is the deep country. As I check my knife underneath my pillow I eventually fall asleep as I lay thinking about my marriage.

Marriage is a "great" mystery

[2]*"A marriage may be made in heaven, but the maintenance must be done on earth."–After You Say I Do*

The Apostle Paul said, "Marriage is a great mystery" (Ephesians 5:32). Our entire existence is about marriage, and yet, for many of us having and maintaining a healthy God-ordained marriage is a struggle. I understand not everyone will marry; the apostle Paul, who was single, says, , *7 I wish that all of you were as I am. But each of you has your own gift from God; one has this gift, another has that. (1 Corinthians 7:7) NIV*

For the Christian, whether married or not, are spiritually married to Christ. God started with marriage in the Garden (Genesis 2:24,25), and He will end with marriage at the Marriage Supper (Revelation 19:6-9). Marriage means union, two people coming together as one, two lives beginning one new life and identity. Even McDonald's food chain giant is a union of marriage. They find business partners to come in union with a system that is proven. Each partner must become one with their business model and they must sign legal binding documents before they can (marry) into that system.

From the beginning, God had a model for marriage and it was a proven system because He established it in heaven with His Son and His Bride the Church before the foundations of the world. All aspects of human life in society must come into some union to co-exist. The government is in association with its people while politicians are in

---

2 H. Norman Wright, *After You Say "I Do" Devotional: Meditations for Every Couple,* p. 106, Harvest House Publishers, 2000

union with their voters. Again, God from the beginning started with a marriage and He will end with marriage when Christ comes back for His bride. Therefore, God hates divorce, which we will discuss later; it unplugs all that He intended marriage to be. It corrupts His plan on so many levels. Sin did not take God by surprise and He knew corrupt men would want to divorce God, He knew men would divorce their wives. Therefore, before the foundation of the world God had a backup plan, a plan to reconcile, to reunite God and man through His Son Jesus with a sacrificial wedding ceremony. We will discuss more on marriage in the upcoming chapters.

[3]*Paul Frost once said that,* ***"A successful marriage demands a divorce: a divorce from your own self love!"***

[3] Sandra Maddox, *"Growing Old Together"*, The art of Domesticity, August, 2013, February 2020

Chapter Two
THAT WOMAN "YOU" GAVE ME!

"A man can fail many times, but he isn't a failure until he begins to blame somebody else." -John Burroughs, American Naturalist

"Then the man said, "The woman whom You gave to be with me, she gave me of the tree, and I ate." (Genesis 3:12) NIV

To Blame is to Be-little!

That evening at the ranch, before I fell asleep I'm thinking, "Where did I go wrong? Is it my fault or hers?" For over four thousand years men and women have clamored where the blame is placed for the Fall of humanity, on Adam or Eve! But the Bible is clear: Adam is to blame; he is the corporate head of all Mankind. (1 Timothy 2:14) *"And Adam was not deceived, but the woman being deceived, fell into transgression."*

Before the Fall, Adam understood Eve to be his wife, bone of his bone, flesh of his flesh, not merely a woman. But after the Fall he called Eve *the woman You gave me,* because he has devalued her and blames her for his inadequacies. That's what ungodly husbands do, belittle their wives because it's easier to blame than to accept one's own failures.

A counselor once told me he counseled a husband and wife about their marriage; the wife explained, after several attempts to get her husband to spend more time with her, take her dancing, and going out to dinner, etc., the husband ignored her plea and made excuses why he couldn't oblige her request. You've heard them before, perhaps used them yourself; "I have work from the office to catch up with; I have a deadline to meet; I'm too tired; or, I promise next week." In counseling the husband admitted he dropped the ball by not listening and ignoring his wife, and not picking up the signs she gave. However, the husband could not stop blaming his wife for their comatose marriage. He would say, *"I know I dropped the ball, but if she had explained how important it was for us to do those things I would have responded better."* He blamed his wife for His laziness and selfishness and for not doing a better job of getting him to understand her. (1 Peter 3:7) says it's the husband's responsibility to dwell with their wives with understanding, not the other way around.

Though the husband is usually the reason for an unhappy marriage, there are times wives will blame their husbands for her misguided dissatisfaction in the marriage. In (Genesis 30:1,2), Rachel, the wife of Jacob, is in a state of despair, even to the point of death, she thought. Jacob, who loved Rachel with all his heart, is also married to Rachel's older sister Leah, huh! Jacob was tricked into marrying Leah, the daughter of Laban, a manipulative man who always looked to advance his fortune even at the cost of his daughters.

As the story goes, after twenty years in a foreign land Jacob sets out to find a wife from his people. As he approaches a well of water in his father's land a beautiful woman comes to water her father's sheep; it turns out, it is Rachel, his first cousin whom he'd never met. *Don't cringe in judgment; you probably have a first-cousin marriage in your family somewhere too. lol!*

Jacob sees her and tries to impress her by moving a large stone that covers the well. He becomes so smitten and inebriated with her beauty he falls desperately in love and begins to cry. "Wait–what! -He cries?" He meets her father, Laban and says he wants to marry Rachel. Laban asks, which was their custom, "What will you give me for her?" Jacob says I will work for you for seven years without pay. ***Now that is love at first sight!***

Laban agrees and says I want to celebrate with a feast tonight for this grand occasion and will send my daughter to you tonight to consummate the marriage. Sometime late that night after everyone has feasted and probably drunk, including Jacob, Laban sends his older daughter into Jacobs tent not Rachel the one he thinks he is marrying. The next morning Jacob realizes he has slept with and married Leah, the not so beautiful one. He runs to Laban, "What have you done? Why have you tricked me?" Laban makes up some jive story, "It is our custom that the older daughter must be given in marriage first." Jacob is so obsessed with Rachel, he says, "What do I need to do to marry Rachel?" Laban says, give me another seven years... and you know what? He does! Finally, after fourteen years of working "without pay," Jacob leaves with his two wives, and Leah bears Jacob four sons and Rachel remains barren. Though Jacob loved Rachel more she feels inadequate, devalued, and diminished in her own eyes because she is childless. She becomes envious of her sister and tells Jacob to *"Give me a child or I will die."* He becomes angry for he has preferred Rachel over Leah; he has loved her over her sister. He says, *"Am I in the place of God, who has withheld from you the fruit of your womb?"* She blames her husband for her situation, but in this case, he is not to blame. Sometimes it's hard to look past our pain and see the love our spouses demonstrate; their love is overshadowed in our grief, and we only see their flaws.

Most people will blame others when they have lost control, they try and gain power by placing blame on the other person by making them feel bad or guilty. This is usually a learned behavior picked up from their parents. Other reasons why we blame or refuse to take responsibility for our own mistakes or unwilling to accept a traumatic event we have caused, as a reality, is because we suppress it to excuse our behavior and alleviate the pain of guilt. By blaming others, we trick ourselves into feeling better about our own flawed emotions.

Perhaps the main reason my marriage was failing and the church wasn't growing is because of the blame game. One of the people I *blamed* most [past tense], for the lack of church growth is my wife. I used to think ***before God put a mirror in my face***, "She is the reason why the church is not growing. Her lack of commitment to me and the church, her continuous nagging about what I should not do or not say to the church members, the criticizing of my sermons, her inability not to encourage me and support me has caused a chasm between us and it has not gone unnoticed by the congregation. Although we are polite to one another at church we are strangers at home. The church senses the tension and division between my wife and me although they pretend not to, and it causes an uncomfortableness and uncertainty in the church and it's all because of her."

Wow! What an immature and selfish jerk! I can't believe God chose me to pastor His church with an attitude like that!

In retrospect, the devil knows how to corrupt our minds with erroneous thoughts and half-truths about our spouses. He tells us lies and plants little seeds of lies that spring up later when we think the dust has settled. Satan is the "father" of lies; it is the father that carries the seed, and he is a master at impregnating God's people with seeds of untruth and half-truths about our spouses. This is what the serpent did to Eve; he told her half-truths. These lies we believe about our spouse and ourselves can lie dormant and undetected, but spring up quickly when offended.

[4]In his best seller book, "The Lies Couples Believe," – which I highly recommend, Dr. Chris Thurman writes there are ten lies we believe in marriage. I won't list all ten, but there are three that stood out to me.

1. *My spouse is a bigger mess of a human being than I am.*
2. *Our marital problems are all my spouses' fault.*
3. *My spouse should accept me just the way I am.*

[4] Dr. Chris Thurman, *The Lies Couples Believe*, David C Cook-Publishers, 2015, content page

Because of these lies and faulty thinking, I would believe, "We are desperately unequally yoked and I am miserable." I'm sure she felt the same about me.

These are the thoughts and emotions that ran rampant in my mind from time to time; although I must admit these thoughts were not all the seed of Satan, some of these sprang from my own heart's bitterness. Even though I have never told her I blamed her, I could never do that; but my attitude and posture suggested it just the same. I read somewhere once that said, *"It's not what you say, but how you say it."* Yes, it's a cliché, but the expression is right on target, especially when it comes to communicating face to face. The truth is our nonverbal language speaks louder than words. The article cites gestures and body language account for over 93% of what we are trying to convey. The meaning in our messages while talking makes up only 7% of the intent. The purpose of our message comes more from our expressions and gestures than the words we use. I'm not sure how accurate that is, but our body gesture says a lot.

Either way, it is taxing on my mind and heavy on my soul. These are the thoughts that the devil uses to create chaos and disorder in my marriage, family, and church. But I have learned how to cast down anything that tries to exalt itself above the word of God. I no longer allow the devil space in my mind to troll lies about my wife or me because I cast them down when he tries.

Nothing can stand against the Word of God:

2 Corinthians 10:5 tells us we are to, *cast down arguments and every high thing that exalts itself against the knowledge of God, bringing every thought into captivity to the obedience of Christ.*

My interpretation: use whatever lie the devil tries to place in our mind against him*; let his lies trigger God's truth.* God's truth will always "demolish" Satan's lies, for Jesus is the truth and He has already won. Whenever the religious elite tried to twist and trip Jesus up regarding the scriptures, He would say you have erred in the scriptures, and the devil is your father; then he would proceed rightly dividing God's word and put them to such shame they refused to ask Him anymore questions, and began to make up lies about Him.

When Satan personally tried to tempt Jesus into worshiping him, Jesus reminded him of the Word! *"It is written 'Man shall not live by bread alone, but by every word that proceeds from the mouth of God.'" "It is written again, 'You shall not tempt the LORD your God.'"" "Away with you Satan! For it is written, 'You shall worship (your) LORD God, and Him only you shall serve.* Even the devil still serves God. *(Matthew 4:1-11)*

When the enemy says my wife is against me, I say, "Satan, *"My wife shall be as a fruitful vine in the very heart of thy house."* or *"Whoever finds a wife finds a good thing"* ; finally, *"Who can find a virtuous wife? For her worth is far above rubies. The heart of her husband safely trusts her; so he will have no lack of gain. She does him good and not evil all the days of her life."* (Psalm 128:3; Proverbs 18:22; Proverbs 31:10-12).

Then, I become resolute and say, "No weapon formed against my wife and family shall prosper devil, you might try to ***form*** my wife as a weapon against me, but she will not *con*-form, but be *trans*-formed by the renewing of God's word. Or if the enemy says, "You don't have the power, you're too weak, and things will never change in your marriage"; I remind him what Jesus says in (Luke 10:19) Jesus says, *"Behold, I give you the authority to trample on serpents and scorpions, and over all the power of the enemy, and nothing shall by any means hurt you."*

I would pray, "When I am weak, then I am strong; I serve Jesus Christ, and He that is in me is stronger than you; He fights my battles and I am victorious in Him. Remember devil- it was the Son of God that kicked you out of heaven and saw you fall like lightning. He defeated you on the cross and put you to open shame; now I'm kicking you out of our marriage; the Lord rebukes you! Now flee at the name of Jesus."

Although the trial and tribulations can be painful, and the attacks can be menacing, they are serving God's purpose. The devil is God's devil!

Nothing infuriates the devil more than reminding him of his humiliation of defeat by the Son of God.

Martin Luther said, "The best way to drive out the devil, if he will not yield to the texts of scripture, is to jeer and flout him, for he cannot bear scorn." And Thomas More said: "The devil... the prowde spirit... cannot endure to be mocked."

Adam should have put the serpent to shame, but blame, *"The woman you gave me,"* we might say, was the second sin of Adam. He blamed Eve for the failure of his ministry and marriage. Sound familiar? But his failure to protect her, to stand guard against Satan who deceived his wife to get to him, his inability to cover her with authority given to him by God as the *head* was the reason for their fall (1 Corinthians 11:2,3).

Husbands hold the majority of fault when it comes to failure in the marriage. Jesus did not blame His bride "the Church" even though she is responsible for her disobedience and sin; He took charge as head of His bride and simply covered her with His love and with the washing of His word, and strengthened her with His Holy Spirit. Adam was given the first church and family, and he failed to wash Eve with the word; that is evident because she misspoke it, nor did he use it against the serpent, and they fell.

Brothers, if your family appears to be falling apart take your rightful place of authority over it and cover it with prayer, love, counseling, and the word of God; this is the will of God! ***When you put God's word on your situation, your situation must change.*** This is our weapon, the WORD! Nothing can withstand it; all the cosmos must bow down to it; even Satan must flee when he hears it... "Get thee behind Me Satan!!!"

Chapter Three

CALLED, OR NOT CALLED, THAT IS THE QUESTION

To be, or not to be, that is the question:
Whether 'tis nobler in the mind to suffer
The slings and arrows of outrageous fortune,
Or to take arms against a sea of troubles
And by opposing end them.–William Shakespeare

As a pastor, my mind is always filled with thoughts about the care of the sheep, sermon preparation, ministry, and so on. It occupies more time than the layperson would imagine. While on my hiatus at the ranch, simultaneously, I'm searching for answers for my marriage and having doubt about my calling; perhaps the two conflict, or possibly related? I ask God why preachers both small and great are falling or leaving the ministry? The work can certainly be a heavy load; pastors are expected to preach, teach, organize, strategize, visit the sick, mobilize the flock, weddings, funerals, baptize, counsel, connect with other churches, be involved in the community, have a church budget, communicate the church vision and mission statement, train disciples, equip leaders, have a church program, encourage, pray, oversee all the ministries in the church; while most are on a meager salary. Pastors are often put in a glass house by which people can throw rocks, tell lies about you, incite character assassination, devise false accusations, betray and deceive you, take advantage of, misinterpret, misunderstand, challenge and confront you with bad intentions. And this is from their own sheep! I haven't discussed the attack of the enemy, yet. I understand the reason to walk away, but should we? What I'm about to say next is with the utmost respect and compassion for those that have quit the ministry. I'm not talking about retiring or transitioning to a regional or trans-coastal position, or realize pastoring is not their true calling, but those that insist they were called and left; walked away from ministry because the weight and strain were too heavy.

"For the gifts and the calling of God are irrevocable." (Romans 11:29)

I believe, not all were called but chose to pastor as a vocation or perhaps, were encouraged to do it because someone told them they should. Also, most certainly, some come into the pastorate with the wrong motives. They are called wolves in sheep's clothing, and false prophets. These are soon evident and found out, but what about the ones that have good intentions but find themselves overwhelmed, overworked, unprepared and underpaid; stressed, and then resign because of the pressure? Do they have the option to throw in the towel and call it quits? Not if they're truthfully called by God. To be honest, I questioned my own calling at times and while at the ranch I prayed about it because I did not leave my former church in proper protocol. My pastor was going through a tough time in ministry and God called me several months before the disturbance at the church, and I should have obeyed His call then. Here's what happened.

The Unexpected Voice

One day I was on my knees in a small chapel at the hospital praying for my wife and new two-week-old daughter Layla. She had the most beautiful dark-coffee brown eyes, and resembled me, while my two older daughters Brooke and Jade, looked more like their mom. Faith and the new baby had to check back into the hospital because Faith was having some complications.

A year earlier Faith and I lost an unborn child, a son who we named Oran after my father. It was heart-wrenching for both of us as we held our lifeless son in our arms. It's strange, I remember it was a sizable room for a hospital, the lights were somewhat dim, the room was quiet after the nurses left so we could have some privacy. The nurses were very kind and tried to make us as comfortable as possible. After they placed little Oran in my wife's arms, I'm looking at her and my lifeless child from a distance across the room. I don't know how I ended that far away, perhaps the nurses needed space.

As I walk toward my wife sitting in the bed with little Oran, the despair is unbearable. I see his little body twisted up and deformed but his face was perfect, he looked just like my father. Faith finally let's go with tears and hands him to me. I try to be strong, but as I look at his face I see my dad, who passed away a few years earlier and I just can't hold it together. At that moment, I say in a soft voice, almost under my breath, "Dad, he looks just like you." I remember thinking my dad was proud of me. As I clench the baby with both arms, I realize I can't hold my son and wipe away the tears at the same time, so the tears continue flowing. My back is turned from my wife as I'm holding our baby in my arms, trying to shield how broken I was because I can feel her hurt for me, and I didn't want her to see me cry. After a while we called the nurses in to take the baby away. We sat there in the room for some time not saying a word; after that, everything was a blur.

So, this is the reason I am praying in the chapel. I asked God to watch-over my wife and new baby girl, I could not bear to go through another loss of a child. After about 30 minutes, while praying for my wife and daughter's health the Lord impressed upon me in a small still voice and said, "It's time to go." I had been preaching for about seven years, I've spent many times in prayer preparing for messages, praying for the sick, and the usual prayers we pray; however, this inner voice was more precise. At first, I thought the Lord meant it was time to leave the hospital but before I could get off my knees, in my spirit again... "It's time to go."

This time it begins to sink down in my soul and I ask the Lord, "What do you mean it's time to go?" He said, "It's time to leave the church you are attending." This took me by surprise because I was comfortable there. I had served there for 9 years and riding in the second chariot you might say, wasn't a bad gig. I ask the Lord, "Go where? Do what?" He didn't answer me that day, but the ignition button to my call was pushed. I should have obeyed God, and left the church right away, but I didn't, big mistake. I went three months later at a time my pastor needed all the help he could get and up until a few years ago it bothered me quite frankly that I left when I did without his blessing; even though I asked for it. For a long time, the split made me doubtful at times about my call. Was it my own aspiration to the call or was it really the voice of God I heard in the chapel?

Later, I was ordained by my brother who has pastored for 40 years, but not by the pastor I served under at the time. That haunted me for a long while; I would later understand Satan would use the manner in the way I left against me. He would often put thoughts in my head; "That's the reason for a struggling ministry; God is punishing you, it was payback because of my untimely departure."

So, my pastor and my relationship were a little weird for a while. A few years later we reconciled and he was invited to endorse our work as a church, and he did, without hesitation. I will always be grateful to him, he could have held a grudge but he didn't. One thing a preacher should never do is leave his church to pursue ministry without their pastor's or church's blessing unless there's a good reason. I had a good reason which I will explain in a later chapter.

"A double-minded man is unstable in all his ways." (James 1:8)

Perhaps you're questioning your calling or ministry; for whatever reason struggling with "Was I called or not, do I continue or leave it? If God has indeed called you, do you really have a choice? Just a thought.

There are statistics listed on the internet about how pastors are leaving ministry by the droves.

1. [5]**4,000** new churches begin each year and **7,000** churches close.
2. Over **1,500** pastors left the ministry **every month** last year.
3. Over **1,300** pastors were terminated by the local church **each month**, many without cause.
4. Over **3,500** people **a day** left the church last year.

While preachers and pastors are going through times of testing, these statistics might seem or feel valid; however, I don't believe these statistics are factual. I think it's a ploy of the devil to plant "fake news" to get preachers to leave the ministry or not get involved at all.

After all, who better to attack and discourage than the man of God? All statistics can be skewed to say what we want them to say. I've been guilty of some of these quotes myself; without doing the research, but now that I have I believe them to be inaccurate. Admittedly, many pastors may walk away from pastoring, but let's consider the matter further. If you are called by God to pastor His church, can you just quit? Can you walk away from the ALL MIGHTY? If God has called you, He has equipped you to handle any circumstance great or small; to have victory not defeat. Remember, your call is irrevocable and *in [all] things we are more than conquerors through Christ Jesus.* ***It would be unjust of God to call us into war and not give us the ammunition to win the battle.*** We are not called forth as a natural man but a spirit man; filled with the Spirit of the Living God. You are a peculiar people, a holy nation, His own chosen people, ordained by the courts of heaven to fulfill and walk worthy of your calling. The Bible says, *"He is faithful to complete a good work in you."* God will complete what He started, it might take longer than what we expect, because of our misdeeds and actions, but God

[5] George Barna, *Statistics in the Ministry, Newly Revised Statistics,* Statistics provided by The Fuller Institute, Lifeway, Schaeffer Institute of Leadership Development, and Pastoral Care Inc., 2020

will win, and you will win with Him. Nowhere in the Bible, that I can find, those that are called by God, quit! Yes, some wanted too, and even attempted to, but God never let them. (Philippians 1:6).

As workers in the kingdom of God we may feel like quitting. There are many reasons for this feeling. The congregation is not responding to our messages, or maybe we're not seeing any results in our calling, or the deacon board is being uncooperative, and the sheep, well… are being sheep, and we feel unappreciated; or, maybe the threats are from outside through media portrayal, persecution, or even, as in the case of Elijah, a death threat. Whatever the case, as workers in the kingdom of God there are times when the pressures of life and ministry feel too heavy and we are tempted to just quit.

Let us consider Elijah and Jonah, among many others!

Elijah in (1 Kings 19:1-9), Elijah flees for his life from King Ahab and his wife, Jezebel. Jezebel is furious because Elijah killed her twisted, dishonest and corrupt prophets, and she says to Elijah, "By this time tomorrow, you will be just like them, dead." He ran for 100 miles until he came to a broom tree, sat down under it and prayed that he might die. "I have had enough, LORD," he said. "Take my life; I am no better than my ancestors."

The text goes on to say: "*Then he laid down under the tree and fell asleep. All at once an angel touched him and said, "Get up and eat." He looked around, and there by his head was a cake of bread baked over hot coals, and a jar of water. He ate and drank and then lay down again. The angel of the LORD came back a second time and touched him and said, "Get up and eat, for the journey is too much for you." So he got up and ate and drank. Strengthened by that food he traveled forty days and forty nights until he reached Horeb, the mountain of God. There he went into a cave and spent the night.*"

If God called you, He would sustain you. At our lowest times in ministry He is obligated by His own word to lift us up and strengthen us to complete what He has called us to do, even when the body is uncooperative, or the heart is befuddled, a host of angels will be at our side ready to assist, to pick you up. Elijah temporarily lost his trust in God; **real faith is developed when you're willing to sacrifice your life for your calling.** Ministry is filled with ups and downs and that will never change. Elijah was on top of the world in ministry until his life was threatened by Jezebel. He proclaims a drought, and it happened; he worked the miracle of the morsel of bread and jar of oil for the widow and her son; he brings back to life the widow's son; he rained down fire on Mount Carmel, and as stated earlier killed all of Jezebel's prophets and now he is running from this little woman. We all at times lose a little faith; we all want to give up at times, but trust in God, allow Him to feed you His daily bread, to sustain you for tomorrow's journey, for tomorrow has its own problems. In our times of despair, God will always send us bread or water to strengthen and encourage us; it might be in the form of a person calling us at the right time with inspiring words, or a prophetic word that is "accurately" from God, or a sermon that brings hope and clarity, or an illumination while reading His word; even a miraculous event of a raven is not outside God's probability. God will continue to feed us what we need at the time we need it. He has never failed me, ever! And He will never fail you either.

My Own Elijah Moment

I had come to my wits' end in ministry. My wife's argument that I love the church more than I love her and the children has caused great consternation in our marriage. On top of that, working for Mercedes Benz selling cars and pastoring has become a burden; the congregation was shrinking, some have attacked my character: partly because I was arrested and brought up on false criminal charges by an ex-church member, but more about that in chapter 12. Others are constantly criticizing my every word from the pulpit; I felt like Elijah under the broom tree, "just kill me, Lord, I'm ready to die."

One day, I was hurt and mad at God because of all the difficulties happening in my life; in addition, our church had to relocate abruptly. The building we had been leasing for the last eight years is being sold and left us with limited time to find a place to worship.

The last week before we had to relocate there was no place to go. That was the last straw! I told the Lord I was not looking for another building; "I'm done" if You wanted this ministry to continue, You would have to find a location for us. Now, I'm not recommending anyone talk to God that way as if we can tell God, anything. Thanks be to God, He knew my heart and felt my hurt and disappointments. Without much time to find another location I was at the top of my frustration with God, my wife, and the congregation. When you are frustrated and fed up, undue criticism is usually directed at others rather than ourselves.

God Hears Our Heart

During that same week I get a call from Randy, our landlord, he says, "Guess what?" I reply, "What?" he says, "You are never going to believe this!" "What?" I ask. He says, "I just received a call from one of my tenants I've been leasing to for 10 years, they still had 3 years left on their contract, but they called me to tell me they were breaking their contract."

He was furious with the tenant; however, he recognized it was an opportunity for our church. He gave us the first right of refusal. I went to check out the building and it is a mess. It has been used as a Mexican Food Spice manufacturing company and the smell of the spice in the building was so potent it would literally make you choke after a few seconds of entering the building. I was amazed that the employees there could stand it; they had grown used to it, nose blind if you will. I looked around for only a couple of minutes, it was awful, the smell and the set-up and condition of the building were not adequate for a church at all. When I went back outside after catching my breath, somehow, I saw the potential. I knew it would be a lot of work but I fancied myself an amateur architect, that's what I wanted to be when I grew up, I digress.

As I envisioned how it would look, I called Randy and said, "We'll take it." As it turns out, the new church building is only half a mile down the street of the old building and the congregation likes this building better than the one we were in for eight years. God really came through for us, out of nowhere, when it looked like we were closing the doors of A Breath of Praise Community Church, God kept the doors open. I have learned through trials and tribulations God can be a 11:59 pm God; it may not seem He is coming, but He is always on time.

Chapter Four
A Meeting with a Butterfly

Happiness is like a butterfly; the more you chase it, the more it will elude you, but if you turn your attention to other things, it will come and sit softly on your shoulders. -Henry David Thoreau

The next morning, at the ranch I woke up at 4:00 am. I wanted to get an early start in prayer and meditation. I have come to the ranch to hear from God. I ended a three day fast this morning, and the next three days is a time of reflection, to enquire of the Lord what to do about the ministry, my job, but mostly my marriage, it's not healthy; in fact, it's hanging by a thread. After 20 years of marriage, you would think we would have worked it out by now, but the reality is we are drifting further apart and traveling two different paths.

I think I should mention, our marriage problems are not because of adultery, physical abuse, drugs or alcohol addiction, gambling, or anything of that nature. If one of those things were the cause, we would at least have a solid reason for the struggles. To be honest, I don't know why we are at this cliff in our marriage and drifting apart. I have my ideas, and I know spiritually it is Satan's plan, but our pride on both sides is also a contributor. It's the enemy's mission to destroy the family and the only way he can destroy the family he must first destroy the marriage. Satan will not give up, he will not cease, he will not stop; with every tool at his disposal he will use any and every opportunity to manipulate our mind, heart, and flesh. It worked in the Garden, and it is still working today. *Resist the devil and he will flee*; for a time *(James 4:7)*. Even the Son of God had to ward off this tenacious fly continually. Satan will try to wreak havoc on our mind and emotions to cause dissension, discord, distrust, and disunity in the marriage and home. He knows a healthy Jesus-centered family will cause tremendous damage to his kingdom because a Jesus- centered marriage and family represent Satan's defeat and glorifies Christ.

So, our problem marriage is first a spiritual one!

"For we wrestle not against flesh and blood, but against principalities, against powers, against the rulers of the darkness of this world, against spiritual wickedness in high places." (Eph. 6:12)

Because we have allowed Satan to fabricate our minds with "something is wrong with the other person" attitude, and then place blame on the other, our marriage is in danger. No doubt we have our own individual issues, we all do; but that is no reason to bail out on a marriage. Irreconcilable differences are not a reason to quit. Growing apart is not a legitimate reason to walk away. I no longer love her is not valid for divorce, in the eyes of God!

We must learn to see behind the spouse in front of us and recognize the spirit that is influencing them against us. Don't concentrate on the flesh but the spirit of that person. You will never defeat Satan on earth until you defeat him in the spiritual realm!

Don't focus on the symptom, but focus on the cause. If I have a runny nose, a cough, or puffy eyes, they are the symptom of a bigger problem, they are not the cause. The cause is an infection that causes those symptoms to set in. Satan has us fighting the symptoms of our marriage, not the cause; more often than not he is the cause, but our own pride and stubbornness is also a cause. The symptoms are arguments, distrust, hurt feelings and abused emotions. The cause is the dark forces that blind the mind's eye which is your consciousness, your soul, the seat of your self-awareness and emotion that will behave in a carnal manner rather than a spiritual manner when blinded from the truth. This is not the brain, the brain is the physical instrument by which the mind, your conscious thoughts are filtered through. Thoughts are immaterial; in fact, they are spirit. They come from the spiritual realm, both dark and light, heaven and hell, good or bad. Thoughts are not just combinations of past experiences and learned behavior; some are original; this is how inventions and new ideas are born.

In (Matthew 16:17) Jesus says to Peter after he recognizes Him as the Son of God, ***"Blessed are you Simon Bar-Jonah, for flesh and blood, has not revealed this to you, but My Father who is in heaven."*** In other words, this thought did not originate from his conscious mind, God placed it there. In (Luke 22:3,4), it says, *"Then Satan entered Judas, surnamed Iscariot, who was numbered among the twelve." "So he went his way and conferred with the chief priest and captains, how he would betray Him to them."* Judas's thoughts were no longer his, but of the forces of darkness.

Because we are not trained in the power of God's word and how to use it, we fall prey to this line of attack by the enemy and soon think divorce rather than to reinforce the promises of God in our lives.

Our culture has made it too easy to get a divorce, there is no value in our "I do's" anymore, and the paper it is written on is just as worthless.

Jesus says that the only legitimate reason for divorce is adultery. Now before you chastise me, I understand that Jesus is making a broader point, while at the same time holding us accountable to His word. He is certainly not saying if a person is subject to abuse of any kind, whether it be physical, emotional, sexual, or mental, that person should remain in harm's way, that would be contrary to all of scripture. There are other ways to conclude and come to a decision about what to do in these cases.

Jesus is saying if these things can be worked out if forgiveness can occur, and healing and trust can be restored, then that would be the preferred option. Paul, the apostle, gives an addendum to the teaching of Christ. Paul says another reason for divorce is if an unbeliever, one who is not of the faith wants out of the marriage, then divorce is permissible (1 Corinthians 7:15). In other words, if the unbelieving spouse is miserable and wants to end the marriage, let them go, don't hold them in bondage. Keep in mind, he did not say the believer should divorce the unbeliever but the unbeliever should initiate the proceedings. You might be saying to yourself, "Darn it, I thought I had a way out." Sadly, it had crossed my mind because my wife and I had not been on the same page spiritually.

I'm at the ranch to ask God what I should do? What is my contribution to the destruction of our marriage? As head of the home how have I let my wife and children down? This was a self-examination, wrestling with my own demons as it were. I wanted to be open before the Lord, raw with my emotions and weakness. Naked before him in all humility and candor. After all He knows it all already, He has seen the worst of me; my worst sins, and yet with His unconditional love allows me to blurt out, cry out and freak out about my circumstance. In His care is one place I can be uninhibited; ashamed yes, but not unsafe or condemned.

Because of Christ I have direct access to God's throne and I can come to the Father boldly, not arrogantly but bold enough to know He can do something about my cry for help. Through prayer, God's word, and reading multiple Christian books on Marriage, the Holy Spirit has hurled a spear through my ego.

I finally realized I am to blame for the state of our marriage. Of course, my wife is accountable for her own actions to God, but as head of the home according to (1 Corinthians 11), it's my responsibility to lead our family and have a healthy relationship with God and each other. Most husbands have been blinded by the enemy in this. In today's culture men have been delimited to a mindless cartoon character, or to a caricature of Ted Bundy the shoe salesmen that sits on the couch with a beer in one hand and a remote in the other; or they are castrated and ostracized when they present a masculine persona rather than a confused or feminine one. Today's man is clueless as to what to do, think, or behave when it comes to their role as men and husbands. God has made it clear to what man ought to be, and we would do well to hear Him!

So, here I am, waking up to a beautiful morning at the ranch, still a bit dark, but the light is starting to break through. With the window slightly open, the temperature is brisk with a slight breeze. I can hear farm animals, cows, birds, and even roosters in the distance. Still a little unsettled about this spacious empty farmhouse, I get out of bed, quickly and frantically I turn on the light next to the bed and grab my long knife under the pillow as I proceeded to make my rounds throughout the various rooms. I'm a little paranoid about intruders or unfriendly visitors that slipped in overnight, whether slithery things, nocturnal animals or "Sling Blade" people; you remember Billy Bob Thornton, don't you?

All is clear, now I can go to the bathroom safely without any surprises. I return to the bedroom, pick up my Bible and begin to read the book of Psalm. I would read and then pray, read then pray, etc. I usually use this method when I pray for more than an hour and then spend time in meditation. That morning as I was praying, the Lord brought to my mind something I heard on a CD I was listening to on the way to the ranch the day before. I was listening to my favorite teacher, the theologian R.C. Sproul. He was telling a story of how he and his friends were playing golf, and since I too loved the game, I paid close attention to what he was saying.

He proceeded to explain how they approached the green, and he thought to himself, how he wanted to drop the golf ball onto the green with his approach shot, "Like a butterfly with sore feet." Well, I had never heard that expression before, and he explained that he wanted his ball to land on the green softly and stick right next to the hole "Like a butterfly with sore feet." Although I thought that to be an interesting expression, what captivated me more was how that phrase almost brought me to tears, emotions came out of nowhere and I didn't know why, I couldn't explain why I was so emotional. To this day, I can't remember R.C. 's analogy or point he was trying to make, but my mind and heart raced with all kinds of thought as to what this meant to me. God never revealed it the day before while driving down to the ranch, but this morning, He brought it to my attention again.

I asked God to explain to me the meaning, to no avail. Later that morning after breakfast and getting dressed, I went into the massive garage to play with all the toys that men love, Randy had it all.

I wanted to explore the 300-acres, so I put on my hunting camouflage jacket, orange-tinted sunglasses, and jumped on the four-wheeler motorbike and headed out the garage with my black backpack, binoculars, a book I'd been reading, and my big trusted serrated knife; just in case an unwelcome animal had devious ideas. I at least looked the part!

I will never forget how beautiful the day was, it was just as nice as the day before on the drive up but calmer, serene like. The open atmosphere and fresh cool morning air brighten my spirits and ease the tension on my mind. As I ride, I remember paying much attention to the sky, the sun, the trees, flowers, brush, rocks, dirt, weeds, and yes, any critters that might jump out and attack me! What a wimp. As I drove down a path already caused by previous drives, I surveyed the terrain while passing running deer, wild turkeys, snakes, raccoons, armadillos, skunks, and other furry little animals. I was excited but cautious at the same time, for no one knows what lurks in the shadows; didn't want a mountain lion to eat me, even though the largest predator in those parts are coyotes; and I know I can overthrow a coyote. I think.

Finally, after about ten minutes I come to a cliff that overlooks a plateau of a vast flat field, where cows would feed on bales of hay, and deer timidly cross because of hunters. At this time of the year, there was an abundance of beautiful yellow sunflowers that painted the field in awe-inspiring fashion. It's hard to put this kind of serenity and beauty into words; how at that very moment, both earth and humanity seem one. It's as though I was a part of it, belonged with it and it with me. Once again, I hate to admit, my emotions got the best of me, and I just can't figure out why. I'm glad no one was there to see me, thinking "I'm the macho type, I don't cry."

As I explored my way down to the plateau crossing small streams and creeks, I found a spot almost in the center of the field. I wanted to be able to react in time if I heard or saw anything unwelcomed coming toward me. I turned off the ATV-four-wheeler, kick my legs up on the handlebars of the four-wheeler, rest my head on the backpack, and stare into the most enchanting blue sky, and though it's a bit chilly I can feel the warmth of the sun breaking through the nippiness. Large majestic birds, I think hawks, are flying effortlessly in the air, looking for lunch below in the field. As I relax and get comfortable I begin to see a multitude of butterflies dancing in the field, up and down they scurry, darting, and dashing all around me. All of a sudden, I remember the words R.C. Sproul spoke, "Like a butterfly with sore feet," I asked God again to tell me what this meant for me. At that moment, out of what seems like a hundred butterfly, one, and the only one makes its approach toward me. I don't move because I don't want to scare it off. As I lay still on the four-wheeler, the butterfly begins to softly land on my left leg, as if it had sore feet, not in a painful way, but ever so delicately.

I had seen butterflies in the city before but something about this one was different, not only was it spectacular with an array of colors, It seems to have a mission, an assignment to land on my leg. No other butterfly attempted to do so but this one. It sat on my leg and stayed there for about 30 seconds flapping its wings while looking at me; then, the Lord spoke to my heart and said, "This is how I want you to treat your wife. Your words and actions have been abrasive, hard, and heavy toward her. You have not loved her as Christ loves the Church. Now let your words and action land on her as a butterfly with sore feet, softly." After God spoke, the butterfly gently flew away.

At that moment, I felt so ashamed; I felt like an ass! The abrupt realization of this matrimonial crime led me to weep deep in my soul and I asked God to forgive me; He did, but remorse laid heavy upon me throughout the day. Who would think that the statement by R.C. Sproul, which he used for a different illustration, God used His illustration and brought me to my knees? For the next two days on the ranch, I thought and prayed on a number of things, but what affected me most was the butterfly.

Chapter Five

Honoring Your Wife

During a visit to a hospital for the mentally infirm, a visitor asked the Director what the criterion was that defined whether or not a patient should be institutionalized.

"Well," said the Director, "we fill up a bathtub; then we offer a teaspoon, a teacup and a bucket to the patient and ask him or her to empty the bathtub."

"Oh, I understand," said the visitor. "A normal person would use the bucket because it's bigger than the spoon or the teacup.

"No," said the Director, "a normal person would pull the plug. Do you want a bed by the wall or near the window?"

Some things are so simple we miss it!

Husbands honoring their wives should be simple, and yet, our marriages are filled with missed opportunities. Husbands must learn to pull the plug of complacency in this area and drain all the bad habits of disregard and neglect that fill up over time before we end up in a straitjacket of celibacy... if you know what I mean.

After the encounter with the butterfly on the ranch, I realized, all these years, I have not honored my wife. So often, when reciting our wedding vows we concentrate on the husband loving his bride and the bride obeying her husband. Those are the foundation of what a marriage is built upon, according to scripture; but what is erected on the foundation of marriage is husbands knowing and honoring their wife, (1 Peter 3:7) *"Likewise, ye husbands, dwell with [them] according to knowledge, giving honour unto the wife, as unto the weaker vessel, and as being heirs together of the grace of life; that your prayers be not hindered."*

This, as I have discovered while writing this book, is the most essential part of building a long and healthy marriage, a marriage that will weather the storms of life. Honor her! This is where I have fallen way short. I have spent 25 years of our marriage honoring myself, what is most important to me, decisions made for me. I told myself certain choices were for the family but being true to yourself will make you see the lies you tell yourself.

The Apostle Paul says, "Love your wife as your own body" (Eph. 5:28)

In a sense, I have selfishly loved my own body while neglecting her honor. Yes, I have loved her, I would die for her even in our worst moments, but to die for my wife is not a difficult decision, I think men are built that way. To honor her is the real death because it is a daily denying of one's selfish wants, ambitions, and motive. To continuously seek and honestly meet her needs first commands unselfishness and a humbleness most men lack.

The apostle Paul says, *"We must die to one's self, daily" (1 Corinthians 15:31).* This is the key; we don't need seven keys to a successful marriage, only one key is needed to open the door to a healthy marriage; it's *dying to ourselves daily*!

Though we cannot rid ourselves of our bodies on this earth, for the Christian, we should consider ourselves dead to its sin, selfishness is sin, "*Consider yourself to be dead to sin.*" (Romans 6:11). But if we are not careful, we will still serve sin, because sin is selfish and serves itself through our participation. We must kill the flesh daily, put it under our feet. Most Christians and non-Christians alike are ruled by their flesh, they give into its desire, its hunger to serve itself, to love itself. Husbands must learn to subdue his wants for his wife's needs. If she asks you to go shopping with her as the big game is about to start, overcome the urge to say, "But the game is about to start!" Her desire is to be with you- or trick you into paying; either way, she has a need. If the dishes are piled in the sink and have not been washed when both of you arrive home from work, husbands, let's take the initiative to wash them and perhaps serve her a beverage while she unwinds and tells you about her day.

Men love and honor their wives when we put their needs before our wants and when we serve her rather than looking to be served. To honor her is wrapped in serving her. You can't honor your wife the way God wants unless you love her the way God does. Therefore, godly-love is enough when it is cloaked in all that God has produced love to be. God's love isn't like man's love, His thoughts are not as our thoughts. What we think of love falls way short of what God's love demands. Although to honor our wives is a command by God it flows naturally when understood correctly; otherwise, it is difficult to do because our consciousness to do so has not been enlightened yet, our hearts have not been conditioned to do so. It is my prayer and my hope that this chapter and throughout this book, men have their light switch turned on to honor our wives.

Perhaps you believe you have honored your wife, you've bought her diamonds and pearls, given her a nice home and car, built up a retirement plan, and have a hefty life insurance policy. Many wives have these things and yet are miserable in their marriage, some to the point of suicide. You can't buy honor! It only comes by selfless serving.

Honoring your wife comes from a place deep within your soul. It is an intended purpose and a resoluteness to do it. It's loving and treating her as yourself! And men, we love to love ourselves; we indulge ourselves with all the pleasures of life, fulfilling the lust of the flesh. But if we turned that same passion into a holy pursuit toward our wife's fulfillment, sacrificing for her needs before our wants, we would honor her in the way she deserves. The Bible says God took a rib out of Adam and created Eve, Adam then said, *"This is bone of my bone and flesh of my flesh."* In the beginning, Adam got it, he loved Eve as he loved his own body, he honored Eve as bone of his bone; he knew her as flesh of his flesh. To honor your wife must be so entrenched in our heart and mind that to decline or neglect to do so would be equivalent to amputating a part of your own body.

Why is it important to honor our wives? First, because God commands us! Secondly, our prayers are hindered if we don't, and thirdly, (1 Corinthians 11:7) says that *"woman is the glory of man."*

Adam is the image and glory of God, and since Eve was brought forth from Adam, she too bears the image of God because she is Adam in another form.

So, to honor her is to honor himself. Man is the *glory* of God, but a woman is the *glory* of man. When we think about God's glory, we think of the brightness of His splendor, His majesty, His beautiful vast and immense creation as in the cosmos endowed with innumerable dazzlingly lit stars. The heavens and the earth and all that is in it were made to show forth God's glory: His glory is the business card that introduces Him to all that He has created. The long flowing main of a proudly steed as it gallops in the plains, the array of colors on the feathers of a peacock, the stripes on the zebra, the spots on a leopard, the belt on Orion, the rings of Saturn, the billions of colorful galaxies, the blue waves of the sea, the peak snowcap of Mount Everest, the lilies of the fields, the redwood trees of California; or the aurora borealis in the night sky of Alaska, all were created to show forth God's glory.

But more extraordinary than all that, is the summit of God's glory, Man. But the woman is man's glory, she is his brightness created to show forth her husband's glory to all the earth and that which dwells in it. While all of God's creation was good according to Genesis, after he created man, God said it was "very good"; but then He made the woman! Not as an afterthought but as to say, "I can do no better than man... but wait! There's more!" and created Woman…*the glow and splendor of man.* If Man is the glory of God, what creature could be more magnificent than that? Woman! The woman was the last thing the LORD God created; it's as if after creating Eve, God dropped the "mic!", She is our glory and we fade our own glory, which is derived from God when we dishonor our wives.

God wanted Adam to appreciate not only the LORD's glory but his own glory as well, which embodied God's image, and since God is Spirit, He created Eve physically so Adam could experience the fullness of his glory in physical form. Adam saw his own majesty when he looked at Eve, and for the first time when he touched the softness of her skin when he smelled the aroma of her body when he tasted the fruit of her lips; he experienced love and a sensation that pointed to how much God loves him.

When God took Eve from Adam's flesh, He was bringing the inner glow of God's glory out of man, just as the glory of God shines forth through Christ on the Mount of transfiguration. Man cannot fully manifest God's glory without the woman. Man cannot fully know God's love without a Woman. Yes, each person can experience the love of God individually, but I believe marriage intensifies that love. Likewise, Jesus could not fully reveal Himself without God's glory within Him. In a sense, the wife is the mirror by which man sees himself; therefore, he sees God through his wife. It is God's glory that demands respect and honor; it is His glory that distinguishes Him from all of creation; so, since our wives are our glory, husbands should respect, honor, and set her apart and above all others in our lives besides God.

"But how does that look in everyday practical matters?"

1. **Honor**- in its verb form means to "keep doing it", regard with great respect, really listen to her thoughts, and sense the emotion and feeling behind her words. That takes work; it requires studying your wife, putting down the remote and picking up a book on how to love her. Examine what her mood swings are

and react accordingly, and be in continual prayer as Jesus shows us how to love our wives as He loves His Bride... You!

2. **Learn to see the value even in the oddities and quirky things she does:** they may seem silly to us, but it is a part of her makeup from God. For example, whenever my wife and I go out to eat, and we split a meal, without fail, she asks me, "What do you want on the menu?" My reply is, "I'm not sure...Uhm, what do you want?" Really, I know what I want, but I'm trying to be a gentleman. She then replies, "Well, what about the steak?" She knows I love a thick medium-rare juicy steak still sizzling as the waiter places it in front of me, but that's not what she wants. What she really wants is the Lobster, but I'm thinking she has given me a license to order the steak, so I say, "Okay, let's order the steak." Then she says, "Well, wouldn't you like the lobster instead?" In my mind, I'm saying no! I want steak, but I concede, "Okay, lobster it is." Then she says, "But we can order the steak if you want." In the past, this would drive me crazy, I'm a decision-maker, I hate to litigate simple issues. Faith, on the other hand likes to think through, take her time, weigh all the consequences, even when it comes to steak or lobster when she really wants lobster. I now see her oddity as cute, even now while I'm writing this, I'm laughing!
3. **Make her feel she is the most significant person in the room:** I remember one Christmas party we attended. I was a host of a group of businessmen that had a gala each year. Set at a beautiful hotel, the guest was encouraged to dress to impress with a color scheme of black, red, and white to create the atmosphere of the holidays. Delicious food, activities, and dancing were overflowing with a Christmas ambience. Before the event, Faith went to the hairdresser to get her hair and nails fancied up along with all the things women do for this kind of occasion. When we got to the event, the place was filling up with people, my business associates were already there, so I found a table for us

to sit. I was acquainted with some people around the table, but she was not. I asked her if she wanted any refreshments. On my way to get our beverages, I began to socialize and give out cards, doing my network thing. After about twenty minutes, I glance Faith's way and realize I have left her alone. Now ladies, you know before I even finish this story what the outcome is going to be. Each time I checked on my wife I could see she wasn't having a pleasant time at all; finally, I tried to make up for my stupidity by asking her to dance, but she wasn't excited about the proposal and I could sense her reluctance. To her, she felt ignored, put away on a shelf and not very beautiful. Awkwardly, I ask her for a sympathy dance to make *me* feel better for my selfishness. Faith loves to dance, and she was absolutely stunning that night, but all I thought about was networking. It is a wonder this woman is still married to me!

4. **Let her be a part of important decisions**: this is probably my greatest struggle; as I said before, I'm a decision-maker, it has benefited me well throughout my career, but it has not profited me well at home at times. Over our 27 years of marriage, I would make major decisions without consulting my wife. This is the example I saw when I was raised; besides, most men under a false notion, think it shows weakness to involve our wives in major financial decisions, we tell ourselves "We're protecting our wives from a stressful situation." In fact, they don't always want to know the particulars, they mostly want to be informed out of respect. She is willing to give you the reigns if she trusts you to make Godly choices about the family.
5. **Strive to make her your best friend:** men, we can make all kinds of time to play golf with our buddies. We will move heaven and earth to get a good tee time with our best friend. We will get up at 4:00 am to make a three hour trip to go fishing with our pals, but let our wives ask us to go to the market with her to pick vegetables and fruit, or to go shoe shopping, or cook

a meal with her, or walk with her, Isn't it peculiar how tired we are or how much work we need to do at the office or around the house, or become mentally exausted when asked to spend quality time with our wives?

6. **Know her love language:** when she says, "Isn't the stars and moon beautiful tonight, don't say, "Yeah, it's bright enough to go work in the shed." When she says, "Can you rub my feet?" don't say, "Maybe it's those tight shoes you wear." When she says, "I want to cuddle," don't reply after a dinner date, "I'm too stuffed to cuddle."

In his book, [6]*The Five Love Languages,* Gary Chapman tells a story about a couple that found the secret to a healthy marriage through physical touch. He explains early on in the couple's marriage they had grown into a routine of not touching each other for weeks and months, they were both miserable and didn't realize it was their love language.

After about six months of counseling, it was exposed, they both needed physical touch and intimacy. We all do, but some more than others, it was their love language. What's yours?

He gives five primary love languages:

Words of Affirmation- *This is mine by the way!*
Quality Time
Receiving Gifts
Acts of Service
Physical Touch

I remember one time I was looking forward to playing golf with one of my good friends, I hadn't played in months and because I'm

---

6 Gary Chapman, Ph.D., *The Five Love Languages: How to Express Heartfelt Commitment to Your Mate,* Moody Press, 1995

so competitive, I get really pumped up when it comes to competing. We were on the first tee box. My friend Earl had already hit a hook shot into the ruff, so I'm about to get all over him with a 300-yard drive down the middle. I'm standing behind the ball visualizing what a beautiful shot I'm about to hit. I do a few practice swings... I can feel this was going to be the best drive ever. As I approach the ball, I take a deep breath, I gather my thoughts, I see in my mind's eye where I want to hit the ball, just as I start my backswing I hear my phone ring from my golf bag. Usually, I turn it off or put it on vibrate. I tried to ignore it but in the back of my mind I'm thinking it might be the wife. I started a checklist in my mind: "I took out the trash, the kids are at school, I let her know I'm going to play golf; wait, did I forget to wash the dishes? Nope, that's not it". The Holy Spirit said, "Answer the phone," the flesh said let it ring and hit this beautiful long drive. The Holy Spirit won, I answered the phone and Faith says, "What are you doing?" in a calm but investigative way.

I'm thinking, "I can't believe she just asked me that question," "I'm playing golf!" I replied sharply, with an overtone of annoyance. She then asks me, "Can you go pick up Layla, our daughter from school, she has an event she needs to attend?" I ask, "when?" She says, "Now." Have you ever seen those cartoon characters where their heads explode? Mine actually did that day; I was hot! "What do you mean right now? Why can't you pick her up?" She says, "I'm at work," "Well, can't you leave work?" Now she's upset and angry and says, "No, I can't, I'm in a very important meeting."

After we both had a few choice words with each other I picked up my golf clubs, turned to my bud and said: "I have to pick up my daughter from school."

I could have sworn I felt a tear run down my cheek... it wasn't, just sweat from the heat. Morrow of the story, had I known about my daughter's event; I would have scheduled another tee time. Schedule your week out, who's cooking dinner on what night? Who's picking up the kids? What school events are the children involved with, any business trips that week or overtime that week. I realize that seems elementary, but you would be surprised how unorganized a marriage out of balance can be. Whichever way you run your household, put it on paper so there are no surprises if you can help it. Our counselor advised us to have an Organization meeting, Date Night, and a Needs meeting each week.

The second day should be for Date Night. This is the best night! Our marriage counselor suggests we don't talk about anything other than how much fun we are going to have that night, how silly we are going to behave, and how great the food is going to be. No conversation about finance, work, marriage issues, kids, or future plans. Stay in the moment, all attention should be on each other, how beautiful she looks, and how handsome I am. Man, I love date night!

The third day is often the toughest if you have a troubled marriage; it's "Needs night." Each of us is supposed to voice what we *need* from each other. The word "need" is essential, it means- require (something) because it is necessary and imperative; expressing necessity or obligation.

These are exercises and building blocks to a healthy marriage and meeting our obligations. We all have needs: emotional, financial, sexual, spiritual, the need to be respected, the need to be loved or touched, etc... If we listen intently to each other's needs, take our spouses' requests seriously, and do our best to fulfill them for each other. Then you are on your way to a healthy marriage in no time at all.

What makes the needs meeting difficult is unforgiveness, hurt feelings, stubbornness, and pride. In a dysfunctional marriage no one wants to say I'm sorry, forgive me, I was wrong. We tend to throw dirt at our spouse but remember the more dirt you throw the more ground you lose beneath your feet. Most men are not eloquent when it comes to sharing our feelings or needs, we're wired differently, but it will go a long way in helping our wives to trust us when we do. Women, on the other hand, find it more natural to express their feelings and emotions,

God made them that way for a reason, to help husbands with ours and to balance the rearing of raising children.

Our counselor is a genius; I went to his office one day confused and frustrated about our marriage. Faith and I had not talked to each other for some time; we were in one of those cycles of pouting but pretending we were not bothered by the silent treatment we directed toward each other; we were waiting on who would give in first. He suggested I set aside time to talk with her and let her express all her concerns on her heart without making a comment and to listen and be completely silent intently. "Say what?" I thought, "Don't defend my actions, don't tell her where she fell short, or even suggest she is overreacting; you mean, just listen?" I did, and man did she have a lot to say. As I listened I could feel the weight of how disappointed and hurt she was by all my missed opportunities. Listening opened our dialog and the next morning she was her sweet beautiful self again.

He also recommends, and I agree, that the husband takes the lead role of scheduling the meetings and being the first one to say I'm sorry, please forgive me, I was wrong. Men, I know that can hurt sometimes, but if we want to lead let us lead, especially in that area.

These three steps really help our marriage when we do them consistently, without fail every week. Above all, saturate these meetings with prayer, before you start and when you end. I believe, when you put honest sincere prayer on your marriage situation, it must change. No force can withstand a powerful prayer life, though our answer might tarry, wait for the change.

Spiritually, the way to honor your wife is to be aware she is the weaker vessel. (1 Peter 3:7) *"In the same way, you husbands must give honor to your wives. Treat her with understanding as you live together. She may be weaker than you are, but she is your equal partner in God's gift of new life. If you don't treat her as you should, your prayers will not be heard."* NLT

The primary command in 1 Peter is he must *honor* her, and that honoring is shaped by the knowledge she is the weaker vessel, and she is heirs with the husband in the grace of life.

You husband's–Note that the first word in the Greek sentence (indicates emphasis) is **husbands**! Listen up! Treat your wife as precious as a gift from God to be treasured, reassured, protected, and loved with every tender provision being made for her. Remember, she is God's daughter before she is your wife, He knew her first.

Some translations use the word "Likewise": in the Greek-meaning in the same way, of equal degree or manner and denoting perfect agreement; "to do likewise." Husbands are to submit to their command from the Lord to honor and love their wives just as much, even more so, as the wife submits to the husband, and they together submit to one another, coming in perfect agreement. *For how can two come together unless they agree!* Unless or until husband and wife agree in their roles, there will never be unity.

Part of honoring our wives is protecting her. Not honoring her means not esteeming her value which will eventually lead her to others who will appreciate her. If the wife is not esteemed by her husband, then the serpent, in its various forms, will slither in and deceitfully reverence her. This is what the snake did with Eve. He deceived Eve into stepping out of her role as helper and coerce her into thinking God was holding something back from her. Now, she wanted more than to be Adam's wife, she wanted to be like God. Being her husband's glory was no longer palatable; she wanted God's glory. When husbands and wives want to leave their ordained roles, they seek a glory that does not belong to them, as a result, no one gets the glory.

As stated earlier, honoring your wife is to know her. Men just get confused on this one. We think to know our wives, is to know what kind of jewelry she likes, or food she loves, or her shoe size; these are good to know, but what God wants us to know about our wives and what wives desire from their husbands, **is how to sincerely hear her beyond her words.** A husband must learn the art of listening. We must search to listen to her in the manner we search for hearing from God. When our wives feel this kind of effort to listen to her, she feels safe to reveal her inner thoughts and fears which lifts the weight of anxiety from her shoulders she is not designed to carry, she is the weaker vessel in this manner. This is the level of knowledge that God implores us to know about our wives. This takes careful and meaningful study. This is what Satan did; he studied Eve, and he is studying your wife today. Husbands, we must protect our wives and out study Satan! To know her as I know myself, understand her mood swings, sensitivities, priorities, desires, needs, and even what rocks her world during intimacy. Husbands, it can't always be about us in the bedroom.

In 1 Peter 3:7 is Peter's instructions concerning living as godly believers toward one another beginning in the home. The wife is addressed first and then the husband. This is the same order the Apostle Paul uses in Ephesians 5:22-33. Is it because the husbands bear the greater weight to love and honor their wives? Or, because the wives have the more cumbersome duty to submit and adorn themselves with a gentle and quiet spirit? Not sure to be honest! Perhaps, it depends on what area of the marriage it is needed most.

The word "knowledge" is translated as "understanding." Both men and women have difficulty understanding their spouses. It takes commitment and surrender to God's marriage order on the part of both partners to come to a place of sincere understanding. Understanding is the basis for seeing each other's values and respecting each other's differences. Men may be from Mars and women from Venus, but their orbits are designed to come together as one universe and shine brighter together, they are the yin and the yang that governs the cosmic duality of complementing each other. This is not a popular idea among many married couples; most want their individuality, their own lives that occasionally cross paths just to check-in, while at the same time not realizing they have checked out of the marriage. For a husband to treat his wife with understanding, tenderness, and patience, and a wife to respect and submit to her husband, both must be checked in to the marriage, engaged, and determined to be one flesh.

The husband is the leader, and he is to set the tone for the relationship, and a man who honors his wife and puts her first before all, but God, will have a wife that responds in a God-loving order. A man and a woman begin their real relationship when they are married, but whether or not the relationship works is in direct correlation to both the husband and the wife submitting to one another and obeying God's word. These principles are given to believers; however, I believe they work even if your spouse is not a believer, because they are fundamental principles for marriage.

Chapter Six

THE "S" WORD[7]

"For they being ignorant of God's righteousness, and seeking to establish their own righteousness, have not submitted to the righteousness of God." (Romans 10:3)

"True strength lies in submission which permits one to dedicate his life, through devotion, to something beyond himself." John F. Kennedy

About eight years ago, while running a revival in Abilene, Texas, I preached for three days on the authority of Christ in our lives, home, and marriage. The last night I spoke about the *power* and *authority* that comes with a wife submitting to her husband. Well, as you can imagine it caused quite a stir. Submission is not a popular word, even more, it's not a popular concept; it saws against the grain of the flesh and cuts into pride. It's that shrouded word that Christian wives know but are hesitant and guarded in dialogue about it. The S-word has been abused by overzealous and overbearing husbands and tainted what God ordained to be good.

To submit is to surrender! The verb means to *"Cease resistance to an enemy or opponent and submit to their authority."* It goes without saying,

[7] WARNING: If you don't want to be convicted, rebuked or corrected. If you're not ready to totally surrender to God's word, don't read this chapter; skip it and move on.

hardly anyone wants to submit to another person's authority in today's culture, so I was skating on thin ice that evening.

However, a mind provoking paradigm shift in the way we viewed submission transformed and enlightened the congregation that night. The move of God was powerful, the conviction was awe-inspiring upon the people; tears of conviction flowed, and the error of understanding submission was loosed. Both men and women lined up to tell me how their eyes were open to the flawed concepts they understood about submission. It was though a light had been turned on and illuminated the darkness of the true meaning of submission and how it's applied in the institution of marriage. And because the truth of God's word was spoken that night, a widow of great age named mother Herring, a saint who reminded me of Anna in the gospel of Luke who lived and worship in the temple day and night, approached me after the revival and said: "Son, you need to write a book about this because the church has abandoned God in this matter." That was seven years ago. She has gone to be with the Lord since then. It took me a while to get to it. I believe God allowed me to experience some tough challenges in my own marriage to speak genuinely from the heart, and not from marriage books, although they too, have been helpful.

What caused the agitation that evening? Submission!

In today's society and in the church, the word arouses such a negative connotation. It gathers in the mind and heart a sense of uneasiness and awkwardness, and perhaps degradation for today's Christian wives. Again, they don't trust the word submission because men have abused it in various ways against women.

In her book, [8]*The Power of a Praying Husband*, Stormie Omartian, says, "*This may be shocking news to you, but an overwhelming majority*

---

[8] Stormie Omartian, *The Power of a Praying Husband,* Harvest House Publishers, 2014

of wives in my survey said they want to submit to their husbands. They want their husbands to be the head of their home, and they know what the Bible says on submission, and discerning wives want to do what God wants because they understand that God's ways work best."

She then says, *"However, the problem often arises in this area because a wife is afraid to submit to her husband for two reasons:*

Reason #1. Her husband thinks submission is only a noun, and he uses it as a weapon.

Reason #2. Her husband has himself not made the choice in his heart to be fully submitted to God."

She admits that God's word for wives to submit is not based on the husband's worthiness, but wives would be more willing to do so if the husband showed signs of submitting to God, she says.

I'm sure that's true; however in our flesh no one wants to submit to anyone. Submission is unnatural, abnormal, aberrant to our sinful nature. Our Fallen nature intends to rule over, not submit under. When a person submits to another it is either by permissive will or forced will.

Permissive: it is surrendering our will for the benefit of another willingly. In the Biblical context, *hypotassō* is not a bad or degrading thing. It is humbling one's self under the mighty hand of God. To willingly submit, to make a choice to do so for one's own peace of mind and to please God. The husband in his submission to Christ, and the wife in her submission to her husband, must first be to please God, which brings about peace in our soul.

Forced: this can be used primarily as a military term: "to rank under" (*hupo*, "under," *tasso*, "to arrange"). In the military, submission is an absolute. Although it is forced at first, it becomes a lifestyle. No one wants to be forced into submission, that's not true submission, but at first, we might have to force ourselves to submit, until it flows from the heart readily.

[9]Matthew Henry writes: *"There is a mutual submission that Christians owe one to another, condescending to bear one another's burdens: not advancing themselves above others, nor domineering over one another and giving laws to one another".*

He also writes: *"The duty prescribed to wives is submission to their husbands in the Lord, which submission includes the honoring and obeying of them, and that from a principle of love to them. They must do this in compliance with God's authority, who has commanded it, which is doing it as unto the Lord;"*

The love which God demands from the husband on behalf of his wife will make amends for her submission, which God requires from her. Her obedience to submission will draw abundant blessings in return from the Lord which God has made due to her. What I am saying is, when a husband loves his wife as Christ loves the church, the reward is a submissive wife. Likewise, when the wife submits to her husband as unto the Lord, her reward is a husband that loves her as Christ loves her. It is a simple formula, but difficult in practice. All the married people said- Amen!

Another definition: The action or fact of accepting or yielding to a superior force or to the will or authority of another person. The word submit, or submission is usually deemed mandatory or obligatory.

But is this the Biblical definition? In some parts of the Bible, that's precisely what it means, for instance, [10]Jack Wellman writes in his article, *What Is The Biblical Definition of Submission? What Is Christian Submission?*

"Paul writes, *"Let every person be subject to the governing authorities. For there is no authority except God, and those that exist have been instituted by God"* (Rom 13:1), and the reason is that *"whoever resists the*

---

[9] Matthew Henry, Commentary *on the WHOLE BIBLE: Complete and Unabridged,* Hendrickson Publishers, 2000

[10] Jack Wellman, *What Is The Biblical Definition of Submission? What Is Christian Submission?* Patheos, May 21, 2015, February 2020

authorities resists what God has appointed, and those who resist will incur judgment" (Rom 13:2)."

The way I understand this is, whatever law is, as long as it is not immoral or unethical, we should pay to all what is owed to the governing authorities. Whether it be revenue, work, or legalities. Honor to whom honor is owed, work to whom work is owed. That is a general forced submission, but it is a Godly submission. Resisting those in authority is resisting God Himself, and if you aren't submitting to the moral ethical laws of the land, you are not submitting to God. (Rom 13:7)

The reason that Israel was disciplined so often was that she "would not submit" to God (Psalm 81:11,12), *"But My people would not heed my voice, and Israel would have none of Me. So I gave them over to their own stubborn heart, to walk in their own counsel."*

Are we to ***"Be subject for the Lord's sake to every human institution, whether it be to the emperor as supreme, or to governors as sent by him to punish those who do evil and to praise those who do good?"*** (1 Peter 2:13-14). I believe so. In this definition, we do yield to a superior force.

However, that's not the same terminology in (Ephesians 5: 22-24) *"Wives, submit to your own husbands, as to the Lord. [23] For the husband is head of the wife, as also Christ is head of the church; and He is the Savior of the body. [24] Therefore, just as the church is subject to Christ, so let the wives be to their own husbands in everything."*

Jack Wellman also writes, in this same article: "Peter saw submission as a godly thing and wrote in (1 Peter 3:4-6) to the women of the church to "let your adorning be the hidden person of the heart with the imperishable beauty of a gentle and quiet spirit, which in God's sight is very precious. For this is how the holy women who hoped in God used to adorn themselves, by submitting to their own husbands, as Sarah obeyed Abraham, calling him lord. And you are her children if you do good and do not fear anything that is frightening."

He says- "I know of very few Christian women, who are not willing to submit to their husbands if the man loves his wife as Christ loved the church, and was willing to die for her if necessary and living with her in a way as to "give himself up for her" which is commanded of men (Eph 5:25). Nowhere in the Bible is it taught that a woman must submit to anyone other than her own husband. No other man has the right to make a woman submit to him...that is specified only to her husband."

As I read Jack's comments, I wonder if most women feel the same way? Most places I have spoken on the subject, it's not a broadly talked about topic. As it pertains to her husband, submitting doesn't mean that she is anything less than the man...they are co-equals and co-heirs in Christ as Jesus submitted to the Father, but both were co-equally God in all aspects. As the husband, there is no better satisfaction than to surrender to Christ, likewise, when a wife submits to Christ, she should by virtue submit to her husband. ***Submitting to her husband is the test of submission to Christ.***

I am struck by the sentence: *"And you are her children "daughters," if you do good and do not fear anything that is frightening." in (1 Peter 3:4-6).* It makes sense that since we are the children of Abraham by faith, then wives are the daughter of Sarah by submitting in that same spirit by faith. In faith, there is no fear! A Spirit-filled woman will not be fearful of submitting to her husband as Sarah did to Abraham because she trusts God. For a woman to surrender and submit to her husband can be fearful, but if you trust that God will reward you for your obedience, it makes it easier. Although, I hardly believe women will call their husbands "lord" these days!

Early on in our marriage, I certainly tried to use submission as a tool of superiority, I thought I was lord, although Faith wasn't having much of that. I had a dysfunctional view about submission; I didn't have good role models when it came to marriage. My father would often be gone for months at a time leaving my mother to fend for six children by herself without any or little financial, emotional, or spiritual support from him. My father was a stern man and certainly did not love his wife as Christ loves His church, he was far from being a Christian. I never saw him beat my mom but I remember a lot of shouting and arguing between them. It was a volatile relationship. My older brother, who I lived with after my mother died, raised me; he also was not a productive environment on how to love your wife as Christ loved the church. Both he, my father, and I use submission as intimidation or having dominance over our wives. So, submission worked against us rather than for us. ***Submission can be a great enemy or a great equalizer.*** I do want to add that my brother Jerry and his wife Oretha, after fifty years of a dysfunctional marriage, finally have come to a place that is pleasing to the Lord; they love each other more than ever. That's right, it took fifty years! You might be thinking, "I don't think I can wait that long"? Trust in the Lord and take one day at a time.

But where did this resistance to submission originate from? Sure, from our sin nature, but how did it manifest itself in marriage? If God created Eve to be Adam's help-meet and to submit to his authority and at the same time be co-equals in having dominion over the earth and not each other, how did submission become so twisted? The answer is simple actually, but hard to digest. God did it... wait, what? God did it!

Chapter Seven

Submission Part Two-
War Between the Sexes

"It's a thin line between Love and Hate."

Originally, submission was fashioned in Adam and Eve by God and intrinsically flowed freely from the soul. However, after the Fall, everything changed, submission was no longer permissively ordained but forced. In His pronouncement of punishment for their sin, God assigned a curse first to the serpent, then Eve and finally Adam. To Eve the LORD said:

"I will greatly multiply your sorrow and your conception; In pain you shall bring forth children; Your desire shall be for your husband, And he shall rule over you." Genesis 3:16

The key phrase in this verse is, *"you shall desire your husband, and he shall rule over you."* Here lies the proponent of ungodly forced submission. The newly published conservative, evangelical Net Bible translates Genesis 3:16 this way; "To the woman, he said, *"I will greatly increase your labor pains; with pain you will give birth to children.* ***You will want to control your husband****, but he will dominate you."*

Paraphrasing- [11]"Most evangelical conservative commentaries on (Genesis 3:16) definitely favor the interpretation that Eve would have

[11] Precept Austin, *1 Peter 3:1-4 Commentary*, August 21, 2019, February 2020

concealed within her fallen nature to rule over her husband." The desire to rule over, dominate, and be independent of her husband, this in a sense would make her *like God* just as the serpent promised. "This would certainly explain why even the most devout, godly wife would still have a tendency to scoff at God's call for her to submit to her husband".

One pastor had this to say: "In a class I led on "Marriage without Regrets" one meek, mild, godly young woman raised her hand and confessed how during the preceding week's homework on submission, she had experienced "a feeling of resentment rising up from deep within and how this feeling surprised her."

Though we may have come to Christ, our flesh still desires to be god over our lives and others. If we understand the "root cause" of this fleshly reaction from a study of (Genesis 4:7), it at least helps us be aware of where the resistance might originate from.

Submission, for women, this does not come naturally, nor does it come naturally for men because of our fallen nature. So, her desire was to rule her husband. Wives, is this something you struggle with? You want to submit fully but something in you resists the notion! Women usually don't make their husbands submit by force, most are weaker in this fashion; she makes her husband submit through means most men are weak; sex or the lack of, or nagging, or emotional deception, or esteem castration.

The closest contextual use of the same Hebrew word "desire" in (Gen 4:7), where God tells Cain that sin's *desire* is to rule over him but that he must master it. Clearly, the meaning of desire here conveys a negative meaning of sin desiring to rule over, dominate, and control Cain.

Ladies, daughters of Eve, if you say you have never wanted to dominate your husband, you deceive yourselves; and the truth is not in you! (1 John 1:8)

In other words, **The Lord declares a struggle, a conflict between the man and the woman. She will desire to control him, but he will dominate her instead, frustrating the relationship; and the battle between the sexes is waged, and submission becomes a dirty word.**

We can see why marriages are so devastated. Since the Fall, men and women, husband and wife, have been in conflict. In society, women have clamored for equality, and men have done their best to deny them. In the home, men demand respect but are denied it. For humanity, the fight will never end until Christ returns and sets all things back in order.

However, for the Christian husband and wife Christ has already set things back in order in our hearts, *for the kingdom of God is within us*, but we must submit to the order individually to have peace together as one. When will we learn? Or a better question, when will we submit?

In (1 Corinthians 11:1-16), we see submission flowing in a way that brings honor to the Father and is constant and consistent throughout the creation order. Each person is covered by the head.

"But I want you to know that the head of every man is Christ, the head of woman is man, and the head of Christ is God."

Submission Generates a Covering:

This passage (1 Corinthians 11:1-16) has caused intense debate and has become more combustible over the last century. Do women have the right to take part in the service unveiled? Paul's answer is there is an inferior and a superior as it relates to husband and wife, in the sense that man is the head of the household. This is why he should not cover his head, to cover one's head is a sign of submission. And since man is the glory of God and God's authority on earth, he is not to cover his head but to show forth the glory of God. So, using that line of logic, why would the woman cover her head? I believe because she is the glory of man, her authority is subjugated to her husband, and her submission is required. This is a foreign concept in today's culture, but we must view it through the eyeglasses of the first century.

To this day, some eastern women wear the yashmak, which is a long veil reaching from their head to their feet. In Paul's time, the eastern-veil was even more concealing. It came right over the head with only an opening for the eyes and reached right down to the feet. This conveyed the idea of respect and honor for the woman, she would never be seen in public without it. [12]T. W. Davies says, "No. respectable woman in an eastern village or city goes out without it, and, if she does, she is in danger of being misjudged." The veil represented two functions. It was a sign of inferiority as well as protection.

1 Corinthians 11:10 is very difficult to translate. The writer of this article has translated it: "For this reason, a woman ought to retain upon her head the sign that she is under someone else's authority," but the Greek literally means that a woman ought to retain "her authority upon her head."

[13]Sir William Ramsay explains it this way—"In Oriental lands, the veil is the power and honour and dignity of the woman. With the veil on her head she can go anywhere in security and profound respect. She is not seen; it is a mark of thoroughly bad manners to observe a veiled woman in the street. She is alone. The rest of the people around are non-existent to her, as she is to them. She is supreme in the crowd, but without the veil, the woman is a thing of naught, whom anyone may insult. A woman's authority and dignity vanish along with the all-covering veil that she discards."

Could this be the idea Paul is referring too? Possibly, but I don't think it's that complicated. I believe Paul takes us back to the created order, Adam was Eve's head and covering and when she aborted it, she left herself unprotected and was beguiled. Jesus, the second Adam is our husband, He is our head, protection and covering, and as His bride, we are veiled in a sense. He protects us, and His blood covering is a sign that our souls are off-limits to the devil. We, in a sense, should veil ourselves from the fruit of this world, we should not eat from every tree it bares; we are in it, but not of it. The fruit of this world is pleasant to the eyes;

---

[12] T. W. Davies, *Hastings' Dictionary of the Bible*, Charles Schribner Sons, 1963,Williams Barclay, Letters to the Corinthians, p. 115, Westminster John Knox press

[13] Sir William Mitchell Ramsay, *The Cities of St. Paul*, Armstrong and Son Publishers, 1907, p. 204

1 John 2:16 says, *"For all that is in the world—the lust of the flesh, the lust of the eyes, and the pride of life—is not of the Father but is of the world".*

So, we must cover ourselves, as the bride of Christ with the robe of His righteousness and walk with authority and dignity with our Head, Jesus Christ. Though we may be seen walking in the world, we are set apart as His bride. It is an insult to Christ when the devil stares at His bride while she is veiled in His righteousness. In Paul's time, if a woman would go out without her veil, it was a dishonor to her husband. When we, the bride of Christ, go out in the world uncovered with His righteousness we dishonor Him. If we leave our gown of holiness at the church then the devil has permission to gawk at us on the street.

[14]"But John Calvin asked, why is it that he would have women have their heads covered *because of the angels* — for what has this to do with them? Some answer: "Because they are present on occasion of the prayers of believers, and on this account are spectators of unseemliness, should there be any on such occasions." But what need is there for philosophizing with such refinement? We know that angels are in attendance, also, upon Christ as their head, and minister to him. When, therefore, women venture upon such liberties, as to use for themselves the token of authority, they make their baseness manifest to the angels. This, therefore, was said by way of amplifying, as if he had said, "If women uncover their heads, not only Christ but all the angels too, will be witnesses of the outrage." Now he says that, when women assume a higher place than becomes them, they gain this by it — that they discover their impudence in the view of the angels of heaven."

Could this refer to the scene in the Garden? My evaluation of the text: That the husband, with his wife privately or in public or in worship, is her *symbol* of God's authority over her life. She wears the veil of submission that covers her head as evidence she has submitted to her husband, therefore submitted to God. Spiritually, it could mean

[14] John Calvin, *Commentary on 1 Corinthians 11:2-16 Regarding Headcoverings*, Covenanter, July 15th 2015, February, 2020

the righteous angels are removed or no longer responsible for covering women who are married because they are covered by their husbands. As I study the word *power* in this text, *exousia in Greek- one of its definitions is the power of authority (influence) and of right (privilege); the power of rule or government (the power of him whose will and commands must be submitted to by others and obeyed.* So, one thing is clear to my mind, as it pertains to *husband and wife*; the wife is to submit to the governing authority of her husband. Also, it could mean she is covered when she does this duty, and any angel, whether bad, would be by some degree off-limits to her, or good angels, waiting to minister to her if her husband fails in that responsibility.

When a wife submits, she willingly places herself under the protection of "spiritual authority" of her husband, this is what I mean by covering. As Christ places Himself under His Father's covering, and a man puts Himself under Christ covering, the order of protection is aligned.

A closer look at 1 Corinthians 13:7, might help us to understand covering better. What does Paul mean by **love bears all things?** The Greek verb translated **bears** are *stego*, which is derived from a root word, **steg**, which means to *cover or conceal, and* **stege** describes a roof or covering for a building. If love covers all, and husbands are commanded by God to love his wife, it is that love that covers her. ***Stego*** means to block entry of something or hold something within. Husbands can cover their wives if she is willing to submit under the roof of her husband's God-given authority, which can protect her from spiritual attacks on her life. Love bears all things, believes all things, hopes all things, and endures all things pertaining to Christ and His bride. When the husband covers his wife, he holds her within his love and blocks entry to the devil in their marriage. This is only given to the husband, no other man can cover her, not the pastor, the preacher, nor the presbyter, she is not to submit to any other. If a woman is unmarried, then it is the church the body of Christ which Jesus is head that covers her.

Adam did not cover Eve, he did not conceal her from the lure of the serpent, he did not block the poisonous lies the serpent reported to his wife, and he did not keep her closed within the boundaries of God's warning. I can see how this definition of "*love bears all things*" relates to a husband's role as a covenant defender of his marriage partner. Our understanding of commitment to our marriage covenant produces a Spirit-empowered love that **covers over the faults of our covenant partner.** The husband does not shame her in her flaws, or belittle her in her mistakes, he covers her.

HUSBANDS: How are you doing in this area? Remember, you can only genuinely carry this action out through the indwelling of the Holy Spirit and His power. Note also that *stego* "bears" is in the present tense, which indicates that this is to be one's continual or habitual activity! This order of submitting to the husband is not about having the upper hand, nor is it to mean that a woman has no rights or is a second-class citizen. On the contrary, God gives the husband some very serious commands as well:

"Husbands, love your wives, just as Christ also loved the church and gave Himself up for her; [26] that He might sanctify her, having cleansed her by the washing of water with the Word, [27] that He might present to Himself the church in all her glory, having no spot or wrinkle or any such thing; but that she should be holy and blameless." (Eph. 5:25-27). **The husband's Christ-like love allows Jesus to "sanctify" the husband's wife, this too is a type of covering.** Husband, love your wives, just as Christ also loved the church: this is a tall order to fill for the husband. I understand wives submitting to their husbands can be a challenge and seem to be the foulest of the commands, **but to love your wife as Christ loves her, how can a mere man do that?** First, Christ commands us so. Second, Christ has equipped us to do so. Third, we are not mere men, but men of God!

The word *sanctifies* means to bless, consecrate, hallow, dedicate, purify, make holy and sacred, and to set her apart. It is Jesus that sanctifies, but He uses the Holy Spirit in the husband as an instrument to wash and cover his wife with the word of God. Not that a woman needs a husband to be sanctified, or to understand God's word, Jesus can do that all by Himself. However, when a woman marries, Jesus now uses His preordained model of marriage, the husband as His representative to help sanctify the wife. He has charged the husband to this duty, and we have no excuses if we do not comply. This could be why Paul says in (1 Corinthians 14:35) *if a woman wants to learn about something to ask their husbands at home.*

I certainly admit most men, including myself, do not always behave in the character of Christ, and in this case, the woman still has her covering because ultimately Christ is her complete covering, Jesus will not forsake His bride. Even if your husband is not a preacher or pastor, he is commanded by God to wash his bride with the word. He should be able to teach her, but if he is a novice of the word, they can go to church together and be washed with the word of God; in this case I believe the husband is still in compliance until he can lead in this area.

If we understand the headship issue is an issue of order—not value, not who is better or more important, then compliance becomes easier. In the home where the husband is to be the "head," and the wife is to be head with the husband and yet in subjection to him as Christ is head with the Father and yet subject to the Father, and as we are co-laborers with Jesus yet subject to Him, then submission will balance the marriage order. There is a sphere wherein a woman is allowed to exert her authority. *Jesus had authority, but He did not have all authority until He went to the cross for His wife; then He rose with all power in His hands.* In the kingdom of God, submission equates to authority and power. Husbands, without sacrificing our wants for her needs we have limited authority and power to defeat the enemy; but if we do sacrifice ourselves and honor her, and submit to loving her as Christ loves the church, unlimited power is at our disposal to defeat the enemy in our marriage and in our lives.

Wives, ruler of the house:

In one of his letters to Timothy, Paul declares that a woman is to "manage or rule the household" (1 Timothy 5:14). The word manage is also translated "rule." It is in the present tense and is a fairly strong word. To rule, to master, to manage family affairs, it seems to stress that the women have domestic skills and men do not. In other words, the home is the women's domain, it is her place to rule, and a wise husband will appreciate her space, which will produce a restful and content home. The home is her dominion, by which all of her God given gifts are on display. There have been many times I've tried to take on this responsibility without my wife's permission, and most of the time, it doesn't turn out well. It is her domain, and as her husband, I gave her that authority to be in charge, only those in control can give charge to another. She's in charge, but the husband must be in control, he must control his own house well (1 Timothy 3:4). I did not say that women can only be in charge at home... but at home, she's in charge, and it is better for the husband to sit on the corner of a roof top than to scornfully invade her domain.

Another thought, the husband loving his wife as Christ loves the church, is not contingent if the wife submits or not. He is commanded to love her regardless of her conduct; neither is the wife submitting to her husband conditioned on her husband loving her as Christ loves the church; she is commanded to submit. Here lies the problem with most marriages; our roles as husband and wife, as cited in God's word is not subjective. We tend to always subject it to what the other person does or how the other person behaves or acts or reacts. Is this the kind of love God is instructing the husband? Is this the type of submission God tells the wife?

Let me put it to you this way; what if Jesus treated us the same way? what if Jesus said, "If Eric loves me, then I will love him; but if he doesn't submit to My word, then I won't submit to the cross." *"He commanded*

His love toward us while we were yet sinners." God loves us despite our actions, he only has one kind of love, *agape*, unconditional.

I once heard a preacher say, "I love you, and there's nothing you can do about it," that's a God kind of love. If your wife is not respecting you or putting the children ahead of you or spending too much money etc., love her anyway. What I'm about to say may offend, but If your husband hasn't always handled money correctly, is lazy around the house, flirtatious, or disrespectful, or not esteeming you, submit to him anyway. "What!!! Outlandish, crazy, nonsensical, that's just downright foolish!"

I know what I'm saying is not popular, but search the scriptures for yourself, with an honest, Holy Spirit, heart-seeking search, and I think you will find it to be true. We might not like it, we might not even do it, but that doesn't mean it's not true. I did not say that you should submit to anything that causes you to sin or prompts you physical harm, but that you're commanded to submit to your husband and the husband is commanded to love and honor his wife is not predicated on each other's actions or reactions.

Who Changed the Truth into a Lie?

The devil has *changed the truth of God into a lie*; he has made the word submission to be self-loathing, inferior, lesser, or substandard. He doesn't want women to have the power and authority that comes with submission.

Submission identifies a person with Christ, and there is no higher power than that. **The sub-mission of Jesus was His mission from the Father. Sub means beneath, Jesus's mission was carried out beneath the Father on earth.** It was His passion because it was the only way to save mankind. Perhaps ladies, your *sub-mission* is your mission from the Father to help your husband, to help him become what God intended him to be on earth. He cannot do it without you!

I wonder how Christ viewed the word submission. Did He view it as a substandard or second class when He submitted to God the Father?

I don't think so. Jesus only does what the Father does, He only says what the Fathers says, that's true submission. When a person submits, in the kingdom of God, they take on the identity, authority, and power of the one they submit to. And if a man is the head of the woman, and she submits to the administrator, she too becomes the head, not separate heads, but one head. Christ never ceased to be under His Head, and yet He never ceased to be co-equal with His Father. He was always covered by His Father, as is the wife, this is the great mystery of a healthy marriage.

Back to the beginning:

In God's kingdom, submission actually exalts a person back to their original status and position. *Those that are willing to be last will be first; humble yourself under the mighty hand of God, and in due time, He will exalt you.* Wives, when you submit to your husband willingly, God will place you equally in the position of dominion with him; you won't have to fight to regain your God-ordained position, God will exalt you back to your created position. Jesus says to His Father, *"Now restore back to Me My place of glory, for I have finished the work you have given Me," (John 17:4,5)* Jesus submitted, and God placed Him back to His original glory. Wives, when you totally submit to your husband, you have the privilege to ask God to restore you back to your original glory from the beginning.

Eve did not finish her work in the Garden, but through Christ, the Eve's of today can finish her work. Wives must first submit in the Spirit of Christ to be exalted to the status and position that is hers with her husband. I believe every woman has a godly desire and a God-given right to be exalted with her husband, but it will only be attained through submission.

Is it safe to submit?

I believe most women who love the Lord and want to please Him above all else, want to submit to her husband, but don't feel safe in doing so. My wife, for example, is a woman that loves God and wants to adhere to His word. She has an incredibly loving and generous spirit, a quiet, gentle spirit... until I make her mad; even then, she does not rant and rave, but simply shuts down, not in defeat but in restraint; that's when I know the cold shoulder and lonely nights are coming. This is how she has learned to cope with my unloving or selfish actions.

I'm not saying this is the way to handle marriage situations, but at times, I haven't left her much of a choice because of my disregard for her feelings. It is curious how small the hallway gets when the husband and wife are not on speaking terms. We do our best to get as far apart from each other as possible. Have you ever noticed how spacious the bed gets when the husband and wife are not speaking? We cling to the edge of the bed with backs facing each other, using our non-verbal communication skills... Faith is good at that one. "I can't stand you, stay on your side, and I'll stay on mine," though it's not said these thoughts run through our subconscious and are verbalized in our body language. Each time these unfortunate and childish events occur, the wife will feel further detached emotionally, mentally, and physically and less safe to submit to her husband. Most men try to coerce or force their wives to submit by pulling the headship card, or the respect card, without realizing, *if they pull the honor your wife card and love your wife as Christ loves the church card*; a godly wife will have no issues submitting because they feel safe to do so.

Think about it, how can a God-fearing wife not submit, or just about any woman for that matter when she is loved like Christ loves His bride. Husband's, if your wife is not submitting, perhaps you are not loving her the way Christ does? The love of Christ is what compels her to submit to God, and when shown this kind of love, she will submit to her husband. A Christ-centered love is not neglecting or ignoring or disrespecting her but protects, provides, and cares for her in a way that makes her feel safe, encouraged, esteemed, beautiful, and that she is the most important person in your life. Husbands, we must step up our game in loving and honoring our wives, they are precious in God's eyes, and they should be the same in ours. Most of us have not had good role models or examples for marriage but that is no longer an excuse when we are born again into the family of God, because Jesus is now our example. This is not to underestimate or in some way, minimize childhood trauma or suffering caused by our parent's dysfunctional marriage and behavior, but we should be encouraged that it no longer has power over us because of Christ.

Chapter Eight
SUBMISSION TO GOVERNMENT

By now, you might be wearied on the topic of submission, but I believe God's people are destroyed by the lack of knowledge. I think this is Satan's greatest weapon against the children of God and their families. The less we know about submission or have been taught error about submission then our families will be destroyed.

Further proof about submitting to authority gives us authority*:*

Again, there's still an opportunity to skip the rest of this chapter if you don't want to be convicted. and if you're not ready to totally surrender to God's word, don't read the rest of this chapter; skip it and move on.

"[13] Therefore submit yourselves to every ordinance of man for the Lord's sake, whether to the king as supreme, or to governors, as to those who are sent by him for the punishment of evildoers and for the praise of those who do good. For this is the will of God, that by doing good you may put to silence the ignorance of foolish men— as free, yet not using liberty as a cloak for vice, but as bondservants of God. Honor all people. Love the brotherhood. Fear God. Honor the king". (1 Peter 2:13-17) This is a general submission for the benefit of humanity.

As Christians, we are to submit to the laws of our country, even if we think they are unfair unless they violate God's law or until they are changed. Though slavery was the legal institution of human enslavement it violated the teachings of Christ. In today's society, the environment between the police and African Americans is volatile and unpredictable, everyone is walking on pins and needles, neither has respect for the other. Some police officers certainly have contributed to this toxic atmosphere by their inexcusable behavior and actions toward black men, and some black men have been belligerent and disrespectful toward the officer, but as Christians, we must not let the few... pull and tug or tear us away from God's word to submit to the authority. The Black Lives Matter movement garnered much attention to a taboo reality of police brutality, injustice, and racism in this country, and Christians should be sympathetic to the pain of that fact, and at the sametime, all lives matter, and we are all commanded by God to be respectful to authority, and the police officer is called by God to respect and value the dignity of all people, even those of color.

When our young men don't submit to the instructions of the officer, they put themselves in harm's way, not only to be arrested or hurt but killed. Even if some police officers are racist, and ignorant and foolish, even if they treat you harshly, according to God's word we are to submit. As difficult as that is to do, we must find the strength and courage to do so. As an African American man, I have been exposed to unfair treatment by police officers, however, most are cordial and polite, my best friend is a police officer and I respect them for putting their life on the line every day. Racial injustices are still prevalent in society and there is no doubt that this has been exercised through police brutality, resulting in countless needless deaths of young black men in America as well as unfair incarceration.

I was raised to be proud and not let anyone disrespect me. African American fathers had to teach their sons this belief structure, it was a way to protect their son's self-esteem. Sometimes all they had was their self respect. But when self respect turns to disrespect toward another it defeats everything Jesus taught. My heart goes out to all those that have lost their children to senseless police shootings, we must find common decency on both sides. It is one thing for a young male to be confident, and have self-esteem, but it is unbiblical to be proud. I know that statement might take some by surprise but when the word pride is mentioned in the Bible it carries a negative connotation. I came to find that, in the kingdom of God pride is a childish concept. When I became a disciple of Christ, I put away childish things. "When I was a child, I spoke as a child, I understood as a child, I thought as a child; but when I became a man, I put away childish things." 1 Corinthians 13:11. To be a follower of Christ, we must put away prideful things and obey His word.

It is humility God is most pleased with. Humility is the ability to be without pride or arrogance and it is a main character that should be seen in those who follow Jesus Christ. "Humble yourselves before the Lord, and he will lift you up". (John 4:10) NIV

There will be times our flesh will want to retaliate, there will be times you are disrespected, and our pride is bruised and our dignity insulted, we will want to raise up to defend our honor; however, it is not our honor we should be concerned about, but how we defend God's honor byway of our conduct and demeanor. Let's not use our Christian liberty as a cloak to disrespect authority. The Apostle Paul says, "Therefore whoever resists the authority resists the ordinance of God, and those who resist will bring judgment on themselves." (Romans 13:1,2)

But a People will only take so much before they are forced to walk in the flesh of resentment and rage rather than the spirit of submission. If a man can't breathe because another is choking him, he will fight, it is both his instinct and right to do so. It is unwise to judge a People until you have become that People. It is unwise to place a label on a man who cannot breathe until your neck is under the knee challenged with every breath to say, "**I can't breathe.**" If the society today allows wrongs to go unchallenged, the impression is created that those wrongs have the approval tomorrow. (Ecclesiastes 7:7) Oppression makes a wise man mad.

Bigotry ought to force us to reconstruct our thoughts because the only reconstruction worthwhile is a reconstruction of thought.

If prejudice could reason with itself, it would dispel itself. What the people want is very simple. They want an America as good as its promise; that all men are created equal with the right to life, liberty, and the pursuit of happiness. However, it seems, for some, the knee of inequality on their neck has strangled that dream. Christians should be blameless in their cause to stand against police brutality, and innocent of inaction. We are sons of God, amid a crooked and perverse nation, and we are to shine as lights in dark times like these.

Equality is difficult in a wicked nation, but superiority is more painful. The police officer should ***"not think of himself more highly than he ought to think but to think soberly. His authority best serves the people when he uses it to serve the people, not choke the people.***

[15]Martin Luther King Jr., said: *"I've decided that I'm going to do battle for my philosophy. You ought to believe something in life, believe that thing so fervently that you will stand up with it till the end of your days. I can't make myself believe that God wants me to hate. I'm tired of violence. And I'm not going to let my oppressor dictate to me the method I must use. We have a power, a power that can't be found in Molotov cocktails, but we do have a power. Power that cannot be found in bullets and guns, but we have a power. It is a power as old as the insights of Jesus of Nazareth and as modern as the techniques of Mahatma Gandhi."*

Submission to Masters

*"Servants be submissive to your masters with all fear, not only to the good and gentle, but also to the **harsh**. For this is commendable, if because of conscience toward God one endures grief, suffering wrongfully. For what credit is it if, when you are beaten for your faults, you take it patiently? But when you do good and suffer, if you take it patiently, this is commendable*

---

[15] Joseph Wronka, *Human Rights and Social Justice: Social Action and Service for the Helping and Health Professions*, 2nd Edition, Martin Luther King Jr. Publishing, 1987, p. 71-72

before God. For to this, you were called, because Christ also suffered for us, leaving us an example, that you should follow ***His*** *steps." (1 Peter 2:18-21)*

Wait, what! "If I am doing a good work on my job, on time, not causing any problems, not complaining, but humbly going about my business fulfilling my duties, and my boss, for whatever reason calls me in his office and berates me down one side and up the other unjustly; I'm supposed to sit there and take it?" Surely the Apostle is not saying that! According to Paul, that is exactly what we are to do. "Wait a moment, don't I have a right to defend my integrity, to stand up for myself, or even tell my boss he is wrong, and he can kiss my behind... I quit!" You might have a right, but is it the will of God? According to scripture, we are to take it patiently, for it is commendable before God; this is what we are called to do.

One day, while working for a car dealership, the Sales Manager, called me into his office and reprimanded and criticized me for taking a phone call from another customer while engaging in a sale with a customer sitting at my desk. I had only been on the job a couple weeks and duplicating what the other salespeople were doing. This particular manager, for whatever reason, did not favor me at all and tried to discourage me into resigning, expressing very rudely, I was not cut out for sales and I wouldn't last a month. With my feelings hurt, sitting in his office, I could feel the anger in me rise; that anger that takes me to an unchristian place, an uncontrollable burst of "I will kick your —- for talking to me that way." Then, right before I was about to explode, God reminded me of this text in Peter; "To take it patiently, for it is pleasing to God." I must admit, I didn't want to hear God at that moment, but I did, and said to my boss, "Thank you for bringing this to my attention, it's certainly an area I can improve and I will do better next time."

This completely took him by surprise, he was dumbfounded, he was ready for an argument, he didn't know what to say, he tried to scold me more but couldn't. Finally, he said, "Ok, then go back to your desk." I raised from the seat, left the office not letting him see I was furious and almost in tears, my pride and ego were hurt. I remember saying, "God, I trust you!" That's submission! I will admit the incident bothered me all week! At the end of the week I went into his office to look at the sales board, and a new sales manager was sitting in his seat. It turns out they fired him! "God is a rewarder of those that diligently seek Him."

Now let's wrap it up with Abraham and Sarah once more: Submission to Husbands

"Wives, likewise, be submissive to your own husbands, that even if some do not obey the word, they, without a word, may be won by the conduct of their wives, when they observe your chaste conduct accompanied by fear. Do not let your adornment be merely outward—arranging the hair, wearing gold, or putting on fine apparel— rather let it be the hidden person of the heart, with the incorruptible beauty of a gentle and quiet spirit, which is very precious in the sight of God. For in this manner, in former times, the holy women who trusted in God also adorned themselves, being submissive to their own husbands, as Sarah obeyed Abraham, calling him lord, whose daughters you are if you do good and are not afraid with any terror." (1 Peter 3:1-6)

Are you kidding me, she called him lord! That is awesome, how far the holiness has fallen. I'm just kidding ladies, please don't put the book down. I wouldn't even feel comfortable with my wife calling me lord, not that she ever would, mind you.

The point I'm trying to make ladies is, from your heart, do you respect your husband that much? ***Do you treat him with godly respect that allows your heart to say lord to him, even if your mouth would never utter it?*** From the heart, have you submitted to him, even if he is not the spiritual leader of the home? From your heart, even if he has not obeyed God's commandment to love you as Christ loves His church? Have you adorned yourself with chase conduct to draw him to Christ? Are you displaying the powerful beautiful gentle quietness of your spirit to move mountains in your home and marriage? That's true beauty, that's submission, a God kind of beauty which is ***very precious*** in God's sight. That is the kind of spirit that is incorruptible; it can never be corrupted to do anything other than what God's word says. Regardless of the situation, your spirit is strong in meekness, enduring and steadfast; in your quietness you are resolute and determined to defeat the enemy- the devil, not your husband. Ladies, you can when your husband over with this kind of submission, not with demeaning him or controlling and dominating him, that's the work of the flesh, *"For we wrestle not against flesh and blood, but against spiritual wickedness."* You will never force or talk your husband into being what you want him to be. This is not to say you have no say, but it's the way you say it!

One of the godliest, holy women I know once told me how God changed her husband through her obedience to this text. He was a rascal, and early on I'm sure she tried to change her husband her way; however, she was wise enough, spiritual enough [that means mature] to submit to God's word.

Secretly, every day, she would speak over him what she needed from her husband as it pertained to God's word, and God has done great work in her husband. Dr. Carl and Virginia Desmuke are now one of the most potent teachers I know. Wherever they go to preach or teach, they introduce themselves and refer to themselves as "Myself." The husband always says this before he preaches," This is [myself] referring to his wife, that God took out of myself and brought her back to myself, and now I've got myself together." He recognizes, without her, he would not be the anointed man he is today. "*Kind words are a honeycomb, sweet to the soul and healing to the bones.*" (Proverbs 16:24) remember, ladies, you are bone of his bone.

Living a submissive life is living a holy life; whether male or female, husband or wife, it will separate you from this world; because the world does not submit, nor is it holy.

This is an attribute that God identifies himself many times, "Be ye holy, even as I am holy." (Isaiah. 6:1-4) "*And one called to another and said: "Holy, holy, holy is the Lord of hosts; the whole earth is full of his glory!"* This Trisagion of holy, holy, holy is the only time in scripture that any of God's characteristics is said three times together. God's holiness must be important to him; therefore, it should be important to us, *"Be ye holy even as I am holy."*

At times, I see this characteristic in my wife, the beauty of holiness, but along the way some of that beauty has been tarnished with bitterness, and it saddens me that I was the reason for her bitterness. My selfish treatment toward her, my bitter actions toward her, my outburst of anger, have made her bitter toward me. Life and death are in the power of the tongue. *"If you sow corruption, you will reap corruption; if you sow to the spirit you reap the things of the spirit, which is life." (Galatians 6:8)* I have not always been a godly man, so all I knew how to sow were seeds of corruption. What you sow in the ground is what you get during harvest. Just about every bad seed of bitterness in my wife is because I planted it or watered what was buried deep, and lo and behold, at times, the harvest can be plentiful. Bitterness is a seed and if watered will be difficult to up root. Hebrews 12:15 says, *"See to it that no one fails to obtain the grace of God; that no "root of bitterness" springs up and causes trouble, and by it many become defiled;" ESV*

Bitterness defiles your soul and corrupts your emotions, and yet husbands and wives live in marriage with bitterness toward one another, until they become numb of the pain or resentful of each other never tasting prosperity. Jesus teaches to cast all our cares on Him not each other, His yoke is easy, His burden is light. We were never designed to carry bitterness!

Chapter Nine

A FORK IN THE ROAD: MINISTRY OR MAMMON?

**"One day Alice came to a fork in the road and saw a Cheshire cat in a tree. Which road do I take? She asked. "Where do you want to go?" was his response. "I don't know," Alice answered. "Then what does it matter", said the cat. -Alice in Wonderland.*

"*And if it seems evil to you to serve the Lord, choose for yourselves this day whom you will serve, whether the gods which your fathers served that were on the other side of the River, or the gods of the Amorites, in whose land you dwell. But as for me and my house, we will serve the Lord."* Joshua 24:15

At the ranch, I'm thinking why would God call me to plant a church? Planting a church came at the worst time! Struggling financially because my business was losing money, problems were brewing at the church where we were members, my marriage was rocky, and we'd just given birth to our third daughter Layla. In addition, I was still grieving over our unborn son whom we lost to a birth defect a year earlier.

While pregnant, we learned that our son had a rare disease and that he would not live very long after birth. We were faced with a decision; do we allow the baby to be born and watch him suffer or let him be induced from the womb without pain and suffering. Sadly, and with great trepidation, we chose the latter. I take responsibility for the decision, my wife at this time is the most vulnerable I have ever seen her and not sure what to do. Usually, a strong independent woman, she was counting on me in this difficult time. She asked these heartbreaking words, apprehensively, "What should we do?"

Did I make the decision to pardon my pain or the pain of the child? Or, to spare the weight of my wife making that kind of choice, or did I have a more selfish reason? I think all those reasons are valid. To this day, I still struggle with that decision and frequently ask God to forgive me, even though I know He already has, but It's my way of soothing my soul. Though it happens every day, it seems unnatural that a parent should witness the death of their child. It's as though your soul dies; in some ways, I suspect it does. So, the vicissitudes of life were weighing me down at the time God impressed on me to plant a church.

With the birth of our third daughter, Faith was having a hard time breastfeeding Layla which made her very emotional, and I lack the skill to comfort her; I just didn't know what to do, but I should have tried harder to help and comfort her. I should have had more compassion and empathy; I should have been more sensitive to her emotions, but because of my selfishness and probably sexist views, I failed.

As stated earlier, the church we attended was going through turmoil, and I certainly knew nothing about planting a Church. Why would God call me during these turbulent times? All my money was tied up in owning and operating a shoe store. I had been a manager in the shoe business for almost twenty years at this point. I made a decent living but was not getting rich by any stretch of the imagination, but I still had hopes and dreams of being a successful entrepreneur. The problem was, I was not very practical with money but I had a determined spirit. However, a lack of knowledge of owning a business would soon come back to bite. I knew how to manage a store but owning a business is a different ball game.

Although the business was open for six years it drained all my resources. To get above water, Faith, let me charge about ten thousand on her credit card, which I never fully paid her back, and the "nails in the coffin of distrust" in our marriage multiplied. You might be thinking, "What do you mean *her* credit card, and you never paid her back? Isn't it one bank account?" Well, that's not how we rolled in our marriage; she had her bank account, and I had mine. I was responsible for my portion of the bills, and she hers. I realize this is not the "one flesh-ness" God expects, but it's how we functioned at the time because of distrust.

We refinanced the house to pay off the remaining debt, but I was in too deep. Because of my economic deficiency and financial inexperience I started the business under-capitalized, believing God would work it all out. *Sometimes we assign God's name to something He has not ordained, and we call it faith.* I am confident God allowed me to own the business but was impatient and didn't wait until I had the funds to do so. I was using faith as a crutch for bad decisions. God expects us to be good stewards with what He gives us and does not want His people in debt. Unfortunately, I eventually had to face the reality of closing the store. All of my dreams, goals, and the blood sweat and tears I put into it, gone! It was devastating to me. It shook me to the core. The shame and embarrassment of failing, the agony of letting my wife, family and friends down, took me to a low place in my life. I am a person that sees the glass half full; I have always had confidence in my ability to succeed; this time, though, it shattered my confidence; this was a place I had never been or experienced, a feeling of failure and shame I couldn't shake. The problem was my value and significance were tied up in my success or failure of the business. It felt as though I lost a child.

Dr. John Dewey, one of America's most profound philosophers, said that the deepest urge in human nature is "The desire to be important."

Lincoln once began a letter- saying: "Everybody likes a compliment."

William James said: "The deepest principle in human nature is the craving to be appreciated."

No one with pure motives wants to fail or see themselves as a failure. If there was any point in my life that I was broken, that was it. Pastoring for a few months around this time helped me, the ministry was my only beacon of hope; it kept me focused for short periods, long enough to take my mind off my failed business.

As painful as it was to close the store God used it to prepare me for disappointments in ministry. Besides, I did learn more about how to run a business, I learned the hard way, but a good experience for me. Eleven years later, I havee gotten over it because God healed my emotional wounds. Whatever failures you believe you have had in your life, Jesus will heal and deliver you from the yoke, if you let Him. Jesus says...

[8] *Come to Me, all you who labor and are heavy laden, and I will give you rest.* [29] *Take My yoke upon you and learn from Me, for I am* [a]*gentle and lowly in heart, and you will find rest for your souls.* [30] *For My yoke is easy and My burden is light."* (Matthew 11:28-30)

In retrospect, I often asked God why He allowed my business to fail even though He opened doors for me to own the shoe store. It's gut-wrenching for me to admit why it failed; I'm both embarrassed and ashamed, but God revealed to me I was not running the business with integrity. I was inflating the price of my product way too high, not having an honest and balanced scale, as it says in Proverbs 11:1 "*A false balance is an abomination to the Lord: but a just weight is his delight.*" AKJV

Balance brings about a just weight. Anytime things are out of balance, whether it be marriage, family, health, finance, or business, it is not pleasing to God. I wasn't paying my creditors on time, and sometimes not at all, not because I didn't want to, the sales didn't dictate the cash flow to do it and my reputation was depreciating in the industry. What made it so bad is that the name of my business was "Rev. Jordan Shoes and Orthotics." Wait, what!! I placed the title Reverend on the window and didn't manage it with integrity. God will not stand for that from His people. It was a hurtful lesson, but it drew me closer to the Lord. He chastened me and humbled me, and I'm grateful He did; because now, I know how to care for His church with integrity. We've been operating for 13years now, and the church is debt-free.

A painter was hired to paint the exterior of a church.
His practice was to thin the paint so that he could make a larger profit.
As he was painting the church, a torrential rain began to fall and it washed all of the paint off.
Then, as quickly as the rain began, it ended, and the sun came out.
As the painter gazed skyward, he heard a voice from above saying:
"Repaint ! Go, and thin no more."

You might have to think about that one for a moment!

While at the ranch, I'm faced with a dilemma, "How will I pay the bills piling up at home?" Now that the shoe store is closed, should I look for a fulltime job and go part-time ministry, or should I focus on pastoring full-time? I am seriously seeking God in prayer; I don't know what to do. About two hours, maybe three, after praying my cell phone rings; I hesitate to answer it because I'm in meditation, but I look at the number in case it's my wife. Even though I am upset with her, it might be an emergency. However, it's a call from Lexus of Austin, I applied there three months earlier. I'd never sold cars before, so I wasn't expecting a call back, even though I was quite impressive in the interview, I must say. This was the most coveted gig in the car industry at the time. "Why would they hire me with no experience" I thought. The only reason I interviewed there is because the owner of the dealership came into the "Brook Brothers" Outlet where I worked part-time and bought four suits and was very impressed with my selling skills. He said it was the best buying experience he has ever had. At that point, I wasn't aware he was the owner; he then said, "I rarely do this, but here's my card." If you like, call the dealership and set up an interview with my manager." I said, "Thank you, I will." It took me several weeks to call, I was somewhat intimidated to be honest. This was a high-profile job selling expensive luxury cars. At Lexus of Austin, every day they negotiated deals with highly educated people, multi-millionaires, movie stars, professional athletes and so on. So, I answer the call, and the manager says they would like for me to come for an interview. I explained I was out of town, and I would touch base with them when I got back in town... I was playing hardball: it worked. They hired me with two conditions I petitioned for. I couldn't work on Sundays or Wednesday, and I couldn't come in on my days off, because I pastored a church, they agreed, which is rare for the car business.

Did God answer my prayer about my finances by taking the job while being a part-time pastor, or was it the devil's ploy? Was I choosing mammon over ministry? I don't know really; it could have been a setup from Satan to distract me from my calling, or God could have allowed me to take the job for a short time; it paid very well and it helped me get out of some financial stress. Either way, it was very peculiar getting that call two hours after praying for a financial solution. I worked at the dealership for four years, until God made it clear it was time for full time ministry. But how could that work, we only had 55 members; the most the church could pay me was about $30,000, I was making $150,000 at the car dealership, the numbers didn't add up!

Two Fish and a Loaf of Bread:

I have preached that sermon a few times over 15 years of preaching, and I thought I understood the miracle of Jesus feeding five thousand people with two fish and five loaves of bread. And I suppose I did to some degree but leaving the car industry to full time ministry would be a $120,000 reduction in earnings. Would I literally live on sardines and bread? Or Pork and Beans and Weenies? Another "nail of distrust" in our marriage because I did not discuss it with my wife before quitting such a high-income job. I just did it, believing it was what God wanted me to do. I don't know how God does it, but for over two years, the bills were getting paid, barely, but paid, every month was a nail biter, and it put a lot of pressure on me at the time. Then, we fell behind on the bills. Faith was not excited about the financial situation, and I got it, no wife should have to worry about the lights being turned off. I put us in this situation not her. Soon my faith began to fade, not because of my wife but because I didn't trust God and probably because I left the job sooner than God wanted me to.

Though the situation looked insurmountable, God sustained us, but it bugged me not to work a fulltime job while we were falling behind financially. It was a struggle, "should I build "tents" while pastoring, or spend more time in the tabernacle of prayer?" I thought the church would grow now that I was a full time pastor, but attendance remained the same. Maybe I chose the wrong road, or perhaps I'm not supposed to pastor. I was walking with my eyes, not my faith, and doubt crept in. The devil really played mind games with me during this time. Finally, after about a year- in- a half, if the truth be told, I simply lost faith and went back to work at another car dealership.

I was on my way home one day and passed a Mercedes Benz dealership very close to our house, about seven minutes away, I thought, "I'll go by and put in an application." I didn't know if they were hiring or not, but what the heck. It so happens they are hiring; they want to interview me while I'm there. I go to a conference room, and multiple managers take turns interviewing me. After the interviews were over, the General Manager comes in and says they want to hire me that day. I accept the position, and all is well with my mind, but not my spirit.

I knew I had failed God's test of faith, but because of His grace, He once again allowed me to be bi-vocational for a while. While at Mercedes Benz, I led two people to Christ. I was often asked to pray for people who worked there and counsel others who had complaints about their job, but soon the tug and call to pastor were too strong, and it was divinely confirmed again to trust Him for full-time ministry. At this point, you might think me fickle about what God wanted me to do; there's some truth to that; however, this time, a divine confirmation was sent, and it undoubtedly convinced me that I would work for the Lord until He calls me home. No going back to the secular job market this time.

Chapter Ten

FROM TRAGEDY COMES MY TRAJECTORY

"Whether our life has been a triumph or tragedy can only be judged at its very end." -Senora Roy

"Now see that I, even I, am He, And there is no God besides Me; I kill and I make alive;

I wound and I heal; Nor is there any who can deliver from My hand." (Deuteromony 32:39)

At the ranch, I'm sitting in an old rocking chair on the front porch covered with a blanket, I can feel the early rays of the sun penetrating the morning blue sky, slowly warming up the cold mist and chill in the air. I reflect on my childhood and begin to think about my mother. When I was five years old, I would wake up excited about watching Saturday morning cartoons. At that age this is your whole world, Captain Crunch cereal, and cartoons. We lived in an area known as Sunny Side in Houston, TX. At one time, it was considered a well-to-do neighborhood but declined over the years when Caucasians and Jews moved out and took their money with them, my father exclaimed! This left the African American community "Up the creek without a paddle," he thought. He said, at the time, Sunny Side is considered to be one of the most dangerous neighborhoods in the U.S. It was a place of violence, gangs, drugs, etc., which produce an atmosphere and environment of crime, social unjust and illiteracy; "not so sunny." We live in a two-bedroom apartment complex, not luxurious at all, but as I remember it, comfortable, but it's all I have known.

My sister Yvonne, we call her Susie because of the popular Everly Brothers song "Little Susie,"; told me later in life stories how rats as big as cats would run on top of the headboard of the bed at night and rock the bed as they scurried across. I'm sure that's a bit of an exaggeration, but it makes for great storytelling. I'm told, a man tried to rob us in the middle of the night by climbing through the bedroom window; he picked the wrong night, my dad was home that night between runs on His job. My father did not play, a very serious man, and seemed to be afraid of nothing. Standing at only 5' 6" he wasn't very intimidating by physical appearance, but daunting when angered with calculating vengeance. As the thief climbed halfway through the window in the middle of the night, he was greeted with a bullet from a 357-magnum handgun that barely missed. My father was an excellent marksman, he must have been a little drunk that night, the man is lucky to have escaped with his life. Dad was a self-educated man, extraordinarily well-read and seemed to be an expert on just about any subject. A very stand-offish and private person most of the time, but when it came to the ladies, very charismatic. He was a good-looking man, mixed with African American, Caucasian, and Indian descent. Everyone says I look just like my father... in case you missed that last sentence, *I looked like my father*, lol! But I stand 5'10 1/2 and the tallest in our family.

I was born the youngest of nine children. Susie is four years older and was considered the darling of the family, but I eased into that title when I came along.

Five brothers, three sisters, and me are the genders that make up our dysfunctional family. At this stage of our family dynamics, only four children and my mom live in the two-bedroom apartment. My dad worked for the railroad and was hardly home, other reasons for his absence was a factor as well but we'll discuss that later. My two teenage brothers live in the apartment but rarely there. They ran the streets mostly and I can't recall seeing them at home very much. Oran Jr., named after my dad, was the soft-spoken and gentle one, he pretty much stayed to himself and out of trouble but loves to smoke weed. My dad described him as a good but scary child. Although my father speaks well of Oran Jr., there's an undertone of suspicion in his voice when he talks of him. Then there was Clarence Curtis who we called C.C, named after my mother's father. I am convinced he was born with a dispensation toward a life of crime. My father told me when C.C. was a toddler; he would curl up in a fetal position and rock back and forth with his thumb in his mouth for hours not speaking to anyone. Reasons why my father didn't care for C.C. would become evident to me later in life. In fact, he said he hated C.C because he was a troubled child and the cops would always come to our house looking for him. But how can you hate your own child? Was he my father's child? There are many reasons for our dysfunctional family. As far as I know, there wasn't any physical or sexual abuse, no one in the family ever accused either of my parents of that. However, my dad could be quick-tempered, but rarely whipped any of us, especially me. I only recall one spanking from my father, he usually didn't have to, his bark was loud and clear.

One time, as the story goes, C.C. wanted to rob a convenience store in the neighborhood and wanted Oran Jr. to help him. Ironically, Oran works at the store, and he would have none of it, remember, "he's the scary one," he told our mother his brother's intentions, but it was too late, C.C. robbed the store anyway and was caught. Because he was a minor he didn't go to prison, but that was the beginning of the end for my brother. He lived a life of crime; drugs, robbery, and murder. He was a criminal, a felon, and seemed soulless, a straight-up thug, as real as one could be. He would later burglarize another store, shoot and kill the owner and received a death row sentence at the age of 21. However, he was clinically deemed insane and would stay on death row until this day. My other brother, Curtis, also lived a life of crime and would later shoot his wife while she was in the hospital. He was high on some kind of drug, probably crack-cocaine because he was shot several times by the security guards at the hospital but still lived. He shot his wife in the head, I believe, and she died. Curtis was sentenced to forty years; however, while in prison, he genuinely gave his life to Jesus and was released on good behavior after serving a twenty-year sentence. After being released and free for about ten years, Curtis was bitten on the face by a stray dog he rescued and taken into his home, his face began to swell and within 48 hours, my brother was dead. Curiously, the doctors could never figure out how or what the cause of death was; it was a strange death, but I believe he died in the Lord.

My middle sister Chris, at the age of 16, fell in love with a pimp and was coerced to move to California, and during that time, someone slipped acid into her drink while at a club. We're pretty sure it was her pimp, Jerome, who she desperately and naively loved. Her mind was never the same after that. She passed away about ten years ago.

My oldest sister Mary Ann married a man she really didn't love, at first, my father told me, but initially, Edward loved her dearly, that would change later in their marriage. They had a tumultuous marriage for years; it turns out Edward was very cruel and beat my sister many times. Though she left him once or twice, she would come back. I'm sure there are reasons beyond my knowledge, and I'm walking in the wrong shoes, but I have a hard time understanding why women do that, but it happens every day. I was told by another woman, usually they do it for the children.

After they had been married for a few years Edward was injured in an accident on his job. Some heavy type of equipment fell on his leg and the use of his leg's mobility became progressively worse. He once told me he felt useless as a man; perhaps this was the reason he beat my sister. I remember seeing the despair in his eyes, helplessness, and hopelessness; or was it torment of the soul for the way he treated his wife. My sister's oldest daughter, Sonja, tells me she remembers those horrible events, and one day her mother said she was fed up with the beatings. She has had enough. He was an alcoholic and would often pass out after drinking many bottles of Colt 45. This time, he pays the price. My sister took a baseball bat and beat him while he was passed out from drinking, broke his hands and left his head so swollen he couldn't see. She said he would never beat her again, and he didn't. A few days later, he drank himself to death.

I remember that day well, I was 17 and living with my sister and her family at the time. I was sleeping that morning and heard a loud shriek; I jumped out of bed to see what the commotion was. As I run toward my sister she has an empty gaze in her eyes; it's as though she's there but has checked out of the reality of the moment. Finally, she says in a shivering voice, "I think Edward is dead." I go into the next room and I will never forget it; the room is cold, I could smell death, not stench but rigor mortis. Though he has only been dead for about four hours, his body was stiff and cold and pale with a morgue-ish bluish tint as I tried to wake him. I felt sorry for my sister, stuck between "He will never beat me again," to a widow with three young children. My sister MaryAnn died about 15 years later.

My oldest brother Renard, I never really knew. He was about twenty-five years older than I was, living his own life by the time I was born. Renard was very intelligent but didn't have a college degree even though he was smarter than most attending college. Our family was too poor to send a child to college. So, he served in the Military and married a well-to-do woman, and at one time, doing well for himself. He had two children but they were never close or had a family bond. He later divorced and lost all he had because of alcohol. Renard loved and respected our father and did his best to gain his affection and approval. He wanted to be just like our dad, so he read books continually and became well-read. He picks up my dad's bad habits, like smoking and drinking and sleeping around. My father was what I like to call a functioning alcoholic; I never saw my father drunk, but as he says, "he always had a buzz." His choice of drink was Gordan's Gin. My father handled the gin well, but Renard, not so much; yet, he wanted to prove to his father he could.

Because he chased after our father's approval he never found his own way and wasted life of great potential my father would tell me. Dad was not very affectionate, but I remember him telling me very sincerely at times he loved me but never hugged any of us that I can recall. He did make it clear to all his children; I was his favorite, perhaps because I was born when he was older in his life and had settled down.

My beautiful mother had straight black hair, she was mixed with Spanish, white, and black heritage, her name was Veo. She didn't seem to be very happy, now that I look back. I don't remember ever seeing her smile, even in the few photos we have of her. My father would later tell me as I got older that their relationship was a turbulent and had a strained marriage. The marriage had been damaged by adulterous relations on both sides. Somehow, it's ingrained in me that my mom committed adultery only because my father worked for the railroad and was on the road most of the time, leaving mother to raise nine children by herself. This had to be heart-breaking and lonely, and it drove her into another man's arms. As a young adult, perhaps, this is my way of defending her honor. Of course, my dad, for sure was a rolling stone, he admitted when I was older. Till this day, we're not quite sure which of the children are his biological children.

Oran Jr. is certainly not my father's child my brother Jerry tells me. What a slap in the face; maybe my mom tried to hide her infidelity by naming him after my dad. Therefore, my dad had a stand-offish relationship with him; He certainly didn't look like my dad, but like another man named "Dusty." What an appropriate name, you can't make this stuff up. "Dusty," perhaps he covered up with dirt, sleeping with my mom, just a thought. I shouldn't blame "Dusty" he only did what most men would do; he is made of dirt after all. My father, who I love dearly, is the reason for their failed marriage.

The majority of the time, it's the man's fault by the way, because we don't love our wives as Christ loves the church. We don't treat them softly as "a butterfly with sore feet." Partly because we were never taught how. Out of the nine children, Renard, MaryAnn, Jerry, Susie and myself, are my father's children I am told by my brother Jerry, who is the patriarch of the family. Curtis, C.C. and my sister Chris are questionable. It's an answer that my mom took to her grave. That is my dysfunctional family. Amazingly, even with the dysfunction, we love one another very much and would drop everything if one of us were in trouble. I would have traveled the road of misfit, criminal or worse if I had been raised in Houston's Sunny Side. Thank God, my trajectory was altered.

The story continues with Saturday morning cartoons and Captain Crunch cereal.

I was sleeping in the bed with my mother when I woke up and climbed over her to start my Saturday routine. Usually, she would get up to pour my favorite cereal, but for some reason, she doesn't this day. I turned on the TV and watched my favorite cartoon, "Speed Racer"; Wow! what a car, however, Racer X, the mysterious character always dressed in black, would show up in the nick of time to help Speed Racer defeat the bad guys, he was my favorite character. As it turns out, Racer X was Speed Racer's mysterious older brother unbeknown to Speed Racer; apparently they had a dysfunctional family also. As I'm watching TV for some time now I can remember my mother not getting up from bed, and I'm hungry.

So, I head to the bedroom anticipating mother has gotten out of bed; she has not. 'Mama get up", I plead, but no reply. As I walk toward the bed, I gently nudge her to get up, she rolls over but no answer. I then say, again, "Mama get up, I'm hungry," but no response. I go into my sister's room to wake her and tell her that mama won't get up. She goes into our mother's bedroom and attempts to wake her, but to no avail. My mother is dead. She died sometime early that morning in her sleep from a brain aneurysm. The thing that sticks in my mind, hauntingly almost, is, when she rolled over as I nudged her, was she still alive? Was there something I could have done to help her?

The next thing I can remember is being alone sitting on the living-room floor watching TV, and all kinds of commotion is taking place, people and neighbors are frantically about, going in and out of the house. Something is off, it is a chaotic scene, I sense confusion and disorientation and a feeling of emptiness and sadness is in the atmosphere, but I can't figure out why. No one has told me that my mother has died. Shortly, a scene I will never forget; I see men clothed in white pushing a bed on wheels, as a five-year-old would describe it; but we know it was a gurney. They go to the back and soon come out with something or someone on it, I couldn't tell at the time. Suddenly, even though I couldn't see who was on it as they rolled the gurney out the door, a sense of despair came over me, something just wasn't right. I can't remember actually crying, but I felt like crying. Still, no one ever told me my mom died that day, it wasn't until my father was called home off his job, Amtrak, a few days later, he then told me.

At five years old, I still didn't understand what that meant, my world didn't comprehend death. A few days later at the funeral, I can see the casket about 20 feet in front of me, but I can't see the body. A lady came over to me and my father, I think it was his sister, she asked if she could take me over to see the body of my mother, my father holding my hand firmly as if to protect me, said "No! He would rather me not remember her that way." I think he did the right thing, and to this day I won't look at anyone in the casket when attending a funeral, not even my dad's when he died.

This is my "Tragedy that led me to my Trajectory." What appeared to be a tragedy, and it was, changed the trajectory of my life. What seemed like a bad situation, turned out for my good. How could that be? How could losing your mother at the age of five be a good thing? Well, the loss itself was tragic, but where it led me was triumphant. I will speak about it in another chapter.

"For I know the plans I have for you," declares the LORD, "plans to prosper you and not to harm you, plans to give you hope and a future." (Jeremiah 29:11) NIV

Chapter Eleven
DOES SIZE REALLY MATTER?

"You would worry a lot less about what people think of you, if you realized how little they do."- Eleanor Roosevelt

"And the Lord added to the church daily such as should be saved." (Acts 2:47)

At the ranch, I ask God why the church wasn't growing. I stepped out on faith and had been obedient to my call, so I was a little disheartened membership had not increased. Was I doing something wrong? Had I offended God in some way, was I indeed called to shepherd God's sheep? I cried out to the Lord for an answer, but none was given to me that day. It wasn't until much later that God has made me understand that size doesn't matter. I finally understood the revelation: the church belongs to the Lord, and He is the One who sovereignly builds His church. I know that seems elementary, but as pastors, we sometimes forget, it's not being social media savvy, or the latest trend in how to make your church grow, or a seven-step process to help increase church traffic. It is not our excellent oratory skill or brilliant teaching, or popular leadership style; it is the Lord that adds to the church. Not that we should ignore data or be knowledgeable to fundamental cultural changes in society, or continue to improve our skills, but always keep before us He adds to the church as He pleases. In some respects, this may or may not have anything to do with our actions, but simply His will.

It is Christ who deals personally with individual churches and her members according to (Revelation, chapter 1-3), but the Father only sees one body, His Son's body, the "Church" whole and complete. In the Father's eyes, we are already perfect "mature," though Jesus is still perfecting us individually through His Holy Spirit and the washing of His word, in fact, the final number of Christ's body is already totaled. He knows all that is His from the beginning. Though we as one body have been sanctified, past, present and future in the spirit, the process of sanctification and edification is ongoing in the natural.

"[12] *For as the body is one and has many members, but all the members of that one body, being many, are one body, so also is Christ.* [13] *For by one Spirit we were all baptized into one body—whether Jews or Greeks, whether slaves or free—and have all been made to drink* [a] *into one Spirit.* [14] *For in fact, the body is not one member but many."* (1 Corinthians 12:12-14)

Ephesians 4: Says- "[12] *for the equipping of the saints for the work of ministry, for the* [a] *edifying of the body of Christ,* [13] *till we all come to the unity of the faith and of the knowledge of the Son of God, to a perfect man, to the measure of the stature of the fullness of Christ;* [14] *that we should no longer be children, tossed to and fro and carried about with every wind of doctrine, by the trickery of men, in the cunning craftiness of deceitful plotting,* [15] *but, speaking the truth in love, may grow up in all things into Him who is the head—Christ—* [16] *from whom the whole body, joined and knit together by- what every joint supplies, according to the effective working by which every part does its share, causes growth of the body for the edifying of itself in love.*

It is every church, both small and great, doing its part that causes growth for Christs' body. The small ministry is as vital as the mega-church because we are all fitted together, we each supply one another and become more effective when we realize we are one body. All true churches of Christ, and every member of His body flows into Him, as all rivers flow into the body of water called the ocean.

So, that means when a member is added to a local church, they are added to ours, they might attend a different *organization*, but it's the same *organism*. If your church has a congregation of 2,000 members, and we have 62 members, we together as an organism have 2,062 members, Yeay!

In the past, I, like so many other small church pastors have an envy problem cloaked in a critique of Mega-churches.

It is said that if we love Christ, we will love his church, regardless of the size. Let's stop arguing about which church size is best and start seeing what's best about each size. When my vision is limited to growing *my* church, instead of participating in what Jesus is doing to build *his* church, there's a tendency to invest our precious resources, both human and material, in the wrong places. How is the pastor of a small church supposed to build a great church if they don't know their church can be both great *and* small?

Since God sees us as one Body, Mega-churches, please feel free to trickle down a portion of Sunday's collections to *we* the smaller church. And the small churches said... AMEN!

[16]On the the hand, it is said: "Much of this criticism is grounded not in theological fidelity but in self-righteousness. When we can point out the flaws of another church, it makes us feel better about the flaws in our church. And what better place to put our bullseye than the church up the road with 12,000 people coming this Sunday?"

My point is that every church has flaws. But it's a lot easier to critique the speck in the eye at other churches than it is to address the rotten logs on our own.

[17]According to the USA Churches Organization, church size does not refer to the physical size of the church building, or the number of seats in the church, or even the number of people who are members of

---

[16] Jay Sanders, *A Rural Pastor's Warning About Mega Churches*, Facts and Trends, October 2, 2017, February 2020

[17] USA Churches Organization, Church Sizes, February 2020

the church. Rather, the church's average weekend attendance; or approximately how many people attend church services on a typical weekend.

Now, we know that's a secular world view, they are studying the organized church, but are not privy to the organism church. They see the seen, not the unseen church, those that are in Christ, not just attending denomination or religion but a part of His body. But for the sake of visual numbers check out their report.

Megachurch:
Average weekend attendance more than 2,000 people
Large church:
Average weekend attendance between 301 and 2,000 people
Medium church:
Average weekend attendance between 51 and 300 people
Small church:
Average weekend attendance 50 or fewer people

God said He would always have a remnant that would proclaim His uncompromising Name. He would have a small group of people that would stand on His word, regardless of the environment, or religious persecution, or popular religious trend. *"Even so then at this present time also there is a remnant according to the election of grace."*, (Romans 11:5). Also, (Revelation 12:17) *"And the dragon was wroth with the woman, and went to make war with the remnant of her seed, which keep the commandments of God and have the testimony of Jesus Christ."*

It is not the number God is pleased with but the church's content, character, and integrity. The seven churches in Revelation are a prime example of God's idea of a healthy and unhealthy church. Again, this is not Mega-Church bashing, I would be a fool to do so. God has not placed me over a Megachurch so I would have limited knowledge about it, but the pressure that comes with a church of 200 people, let alone 20,000 can be insufferable without the assistance of the Holy Spirit and a strong commitment of faith. No one is equipped to do it all themselves.

My good friend, Pastor Fred Moore, told me something I will never forget, he said, "Be careful what you ask for: "The bigger the baby, the bigger the mess!"

I must admit, my flesh and ego have a tendency to desire a big congregation at times, but God is teaching me what my appointment is for now. And even if God chooses never to increase our congregation to 300 or 3,000, I am grateful. *"In everything give thanks: for this is the will of God in Christ Jesus concerning you."* (1 Thessalonians 5:18)

Encouraging the small guys:

In our minds, size does matter, but size can give us a false sense of accomplishment. God is not limited by how many people are in our congregation. He often uses small things for big problems. God will intentionally use less to accomplish more because He wants the glory.

Remember Gideon? Israel is commanded by God to go up against the Midianites; God wants to give the Midianites into the hands of Israel. It is estimated by some scholars that up to 20,000 soldiers employed the Midianite army while Israel had only 12,000 soldiers. Israel was outnumbered by 8,000 soldiers; however, they were the nation of the Most-High God and would have won the battle. But God wanted the glory for His own purpose. He tells Gideon, I will only choose 300 Israelite soldiers to go down against 20,000 of the Midianite army, and that they should not fear because they already have the victory. And so, Israel went down against the Midianite army with 300 men and won the battle. (v9) ***"It happened on the same knight the LORD said to him, "Arise, go down against the camp, for I have delivered it into your hands."*** (Judges 7:1-25) Wow! God is so awesome.

As pastors, leaders, and even church members, we often equate size with success. God equates success with righteous and holy character! Even where there are only two or three, as long as He is in the midst and they agree, all manner of bondage can be loosed, all Goliaths can be slain, all trials can be overcome, all tribulations can turn to triumph, all mountains can be moved. If Jesus is in it, even with two or three, against 20,000,00, we have the majority.

It's not the size of the dog in the fight, it's the size of God in the heart: that's not as poetic as the original, but you get my drift. If a small Church has a huge heart for God, if they hunger and thirst after Him, if they seek first His kingdom and His righteousness, if they have faith as a grain of mustard seed, that God can do with them as much as He can with a large church, God will be pleased; and you will be a successful church and do great things in the kingdom of God. Don't have size envy! Don't try and keep up with the Jakes, Osteen's, or the Jones's; keep up with Jesus right where He has you. Small churches need pastors too!

However, there are reasons why growth may not have taken place in a small church. I will use myself as an example. First, I am at fault. Not because of any egregious sin but because of arrogance and pride. Pastors can be arrogant and impatient; we think, "I'm right, everyone else is wrong, I've been called by God to shepherd the sheep, you haven't." And often, not sincerely listing but mostly talking because what we have to say is more important than what is being said. We blamed others for the lack of church growth because, at times, we see people as lazy, and don't love God as much as we do; or, "I'm more spiritual than you because of my anointing"... man, it can go on and on. I'm not saying I'm guilty of all that, but I can pick out one or two that fits me. What about you?

Assuming the foundation of the church vision is clear, and the church is called by Christ, and doing what Jesus commanded, and the church isn't growing; naturally, we want to know *why*? The first thought most people would think is, there must be sin in the camp. This can certainly be a reason as in the case of Achan's sin in (Joshua chapter 7-9), but sin is not always the reason. Is numerical growth the only sign of a healthy growing church? I would challenge that principle with the example of Apostle Paul's ministry of planting churches small and great. It was the little church of Phillipi that supported Paul's mission the most, and as a result, Paul was able to carry the gospel to the known world. Whereas the larger Corinthian church was full of issues, sin, and had to be rebuked by Paul for not keeping their commitment of giving, and they challenged Paul's authority as an apostle even though he planted the church.

Why is there pressure to have large numbers as a gauge of success? Most of the time it is self-inflicting. When the pastor is rushed to improve membership growth or when he is stimulated by growth, growth, growth, for selfish reasons, and when growth does not occur, the congregation becomes discouraged and begin to think something is wrong with the church or its pastor. Likewise, other pastors, churches, and communities measure their decisions on outward parking lot appearance. If there's only fifteen cars in the parking lot they falsely assume God is not moving in that church, or something must be wrong because in their view the church would be growing.

There was a time when our church had experienced growth over eight months, we grew from 15 people to 65, and it put us in a bit of an awkward situation. We were excited about the growth but was renting a space that will hold 80 people tightly and seat a hundred uncomfortably, particularly in the summertime. If we maxed out at eighty members on Sunday, we would have to find a more substantial spot or go to two services, which would put pressure on a small leadership team. I know God will make a way, but the hardships of growth can be challenging. So, depending on your circumstance, a lack of growth may be God's mercy on you, it's ok to be unmega.

What is the church's most important mission? Make disciples for Christ, not enlarging our local congregation, and not worrying about who comes and goes. As a young pastor, this would bother me; you would spend so much time and investment in people and for whatever reason, usually, they're disgruntled about something and leave. Most would not give you a reason why. Their most quoted line is, "My season is up." Wait! How can you have a season of manifestation when you haven't planted anything? Well, we still must love them coming in and love them going out. Other factors may well play a part in non-growth or slow growth. You may have five churches on one street, as is the case with our church. Square footage and space may be an issue, location, unattractive signage, and church appearance may halt growth. People today want an emotionally charged praise and worship team, special effects, and theatrics. However, I believe those that want more of God want as much of His word as anything else. Statistics say 30 minutes is the attention span for people today and a sermon longer than that, they become distracted. Really? What about going to a two in a half-hour movie, or a three- hour Football game, or playing for hours on video games? People will attend to whatever satisfies the flesh, and they will pay attention for as long as it takes to feed their fleshly desires. Those that hunger and thirst after righteousness are continually hungry and thirsty for God's word. I'm not declaring we need to preach for four hours; I'm suggesting we don't let society dictate how the Holy Spirit uses us in the pulpit.

We should be mindful of areas we can improve. For instance: is your sign eye-catching or obscured? Is your building maintained or dilapidated? Is your parking area welcoming to the guest, or strained to capacity? Are you utilizing social media? These are areas that can be enhanced to reach more people. Also, is it a culture that welcomes with a genuinely warm smile that's excited about a new guest at your church, or satisfied with the members already attending? Is the pastor energetic or boring? Is the church leadership holy or hellish? What about demographics, is your church mission congruent with the needs of the community?

Is your church leadership team and pastor set up as an autocratic system, or does the whole-body feel just as important and equally valued, able to carry out the mission and vision? If the feet feel just as important as the eyes, the body can more easily walk through the trials of ministry. If the arms and fingers are commended as much as the ears and mouth, more work gets done and the load is lighter. (1 Corinthians chapter 12:4-25), "*(v14)- Now the body is not made up of one part but many. If the foot should say, "Because I am not a hand, I do not belong to the body," it would not for that reason cease to be part of the body. And if the ear should say, "Because I am not an eye, I do not belong to the body," it would not for that reason cease to be apart of the body. (V18)- But in fact God as arranged the parts in the body, every one of them, just as he wanted them to be. (v20)- As it is, there are many parts, but one body." NIV*

Do you have people serving in the right place? Is a hand trying to be the foot, is an ear trying to see rather than hearing? Each member has a spiritual gift, but most people are ignorant of what their gifts are, according to apostle Paul 1 Corinthians 12:1. Sometimes pastors will put people in a position just to fill the position or to give a member something to do, but it's not their lane, and eventually, they will cause a wreck. Is the church listening to the Holy Spirit and willing to change its direction if need be, or are you comfortable with the status quo? It is said, over 80 percent of those who drop out of church do so in the first year of their membership. A new member does not automatically become an active member without an intentional plan by the church on how to assimilate them into a caring, loving, Christian community (Ephesians 2:19) *"you are no longer strangers and foreigners, but fellow citizens with the saints and members of the household of God.*

[18]Pastor Charles Arn writes, "There are many reasons why churches don't grow. But there are no good reasons. Healthy churches grow. God wants your church to grow. He created it to grow. Sometimes it's just a matter of finding out what's keeping it from growing and removing those obstacles".

There are three different causes if the pastor is inhibiting the growth of a church: He gives three examples:

1. **"The pastor does not have a PRIORITY.** Churches grow when they have a priority for reaching the unchurched. When the pastor doesn't, the church won't. (observe Luke 19:10)

[18] Charles Arn, *Five Growth Restricting Obstacles*, Apostolic Information Service, January 25 2008, February 2020

2. **The pastor does not have a VISION.** Growing churches have pastors who believe God wants to reach people in their community and assimilate them into the Body. No *vision* for outreach is as much a barrier as no *priority*. (observe Acts 16:9)
3. **The pastor does not have KNOWLEDGE.** Working harder is not the secret to effective outreach. The secret is working *smarter*. Unfortunately, little is taught in most seminaries or Bible schools about how to invest the limited resources of a church for the highest return. (observe Mt. 25:14-30)

But Church members can keep a church from growing too. Perhaps the members have no priority for reaching the lost. "Sure, our church should reach people," some say. "But me? I've got three kids, a job, membership at the health club, and a lawn to mow. Someone else with more time should feel compelled." (observe II Pe. 3:9)

Members have a self-serving attitude about the church. When members believe the priority of the pastor and the church should be to "feed the sheep" who are already in the flock, the message that newcomers hear is: "We like our church just the way it is...which is without you!" (observe Mt. 9:37)

Members fear that new people will destroy their fellowship. When "community" is the number one priority in a church, active membership will not grow beyond 100 people. Beyond that point, members won't know everyone...and, in their minds, that price of growth becomes greater than the benefit. (II Cor. 4:5)"

Chapter Twelve

Wolves in Sheep's Clothing

[15] "Watch out for false prophets. They come to you in sheep's clothing, but inwardly they are ferocious wolves. [16] By their fruit you will recognize them." (Matthew 7:15,16) NIV

"For we wrestle not against flesh and blood, but against principalities, against powers, against the rulers of the darkness of this world, against spiritual wickedness in high places." (Ephesians 6:12)

In ministry, it is often difficult to identify the wolves, but over time they will reveal their true intentions. However, sometimes the damage has been done before we notice. There's a song called "Smiling Faces" song by The Undisputed Truth, which says-

"Smiling faces sometimes pretend to be your friend,
Smiling faces show no traces of the evil that lurks within (can you dig it?)"

Brother, I can dig it!

Nothing discourages the pastor more than an imposter, a person that has only selfish motives. The Bible warns us about brutes of beasts, tares and wheat. Pastoring is a long learning curve. There are so many things to be watchful for. It's imperative to have spiritual discernment and wisdom when walking in the arena of the devil. Satan is the prince of the power of the air, but has restricted range to create chaos wherever he goes; for he came to kill, still, and destroy all of those that march under the banner of Jesus.

When the right crack is opened through sin or doubt or lack of knowledge, or not obeying the warning of the Holy Spirit, the enemy can cause substantial damage.

One evening after a long day I walk in the house exhausted. I throw the keys on the table heading toward my man-cave to begin watching news and sports; the family has already eaten dinner and is winding down for bed. Not sure whether to warm up leftovers or become a sinkhole on the couch, I decided the latter. Trying to relax and forget about the day, my cell phone rings on the dining room table in the other room, I think to myself, "I am not moving, if it is important they will leave a message." After about thirty minutes, I get up to get a glass of cold Ice-tea and check the message; it's from a member that has recently left the church, his wife is still a member but he has resigned his membership. He and his wife have had severe problems in their marriage for years. He has abused her physically and was violent to her and their children, I am told by his wife. At this point, she has decided to separate and move out, but there's also something suspicious about the wife as well, she doesn't seem to be very stable; that's understandable in her situation, but something else is odd and I can't discern what it is. Usually, I can detect bad intentions or mischief, but she was clever at hiding hers. Although she claims to be a minister she has not been a member of our church very long, so it's difficult to get a read on her. One of the spiritual ladies at our church, who has been with me from the beginning, say's, "Pastor, watch out for her, something isn't quite right"; she was picking up something I wasn't.

Ephesians 5:6 says "Let no one deceive you with empty words"; Jeremiah 17:9 says, "The heart is deceitful above all things, And [a] desperately wicked; Who can know it?

"Job 15:35 says, "They conceive trouble and give birth to evil; their womb fashions deceit." NIV

So, as I check the message, it's her husband on the phone, and he is irritated spitting out words, no Christian should be uttering, questioning my manhood and blaming me for his wife moving out. He says I had no right to tell her who they should and should not counsel with, that they can counsel with whomever they wanted to. Well, at this point I'm confused, I haven't got a clue as to what he is referring to. I have never instructed anyone who they should or should not counsel with; where was he getting that information? It seems someone has told him that, I said, they could only advise with me. I had never counseled him or his wife; in fact, when she asked me what she should do about her marriage, I said she should find a professional marriage counselor. Her troubled marriage was beyond my skill level.

When I heard the husband's rude and misinformed message, the Holy Spirit told me in my spirit, "Don't call him back". I hang up the voicemail on the phone and walk back into the den to watch TV. In my mind, the words of the man kept taunting me; to be honest, I was a little offended and insulted. After about twenty minutes or so, pride begins to rise up in me and the other voice, not the Holy Spirit, says "call him just to ask him why he was so angry and why he thought I prohibited him and his wife to counsel with someone other than me?" My offended flesh said to call him, the Holy Spirit said, don't. That night, I let the flesh win. I called the husband and asked him, "Why was he so angry with me?" After he called me names again, he wanted to talk with me in person. I said, "Ok, let's meet at Starbucks." He said, "That would be fine, but he would rather me come to his house." Now, at this point, any pastor should know this situation is too toxic, and either they should meet at a later date when emotions are settled or take another church member with them. I did neither.

I drove over to the man's house, hoping we could clear the matter up. As I approach his front door, he steps out onto the porch. This was odd, he didn't invite me in; he was supposed to be at home alone because his wife has already moved out. Immediately, he becomes agitated and loud and wants to argue. I replied and said, "Brother, I didn't come here to argue, I just wanted you to know you've got the situation all wrong;" then, I see fire in his eyes. "He says wait right here I'll be right back." Obviously, I had a bad feeling and started to make my way back to my car to leave. Before I get to my car he comes out with a baseball bat and stands in front of me and my vehicle. With a crazy look in his eyes, he raises and points the bat at me. He approaches me as if to hit me with the baseball bat. He picks the wrong person to attack; all my life, I have been a fighter, and when my anger reaches a certain point it's all or nothing; either you're going down, or you will have to kill me.

Suddenly, the rage in me reached that point of no return. As he came toward me, I ran toward him, wrapped him up and picked him up, and threw him on the hood of my car. As he tries to hit me with the bat while on the hood of my car, I see blood on my white shirt; I'm thinking it's his blood, but I soon realize I'm bleeding from the top of my head. Then I lost all control, picked him up again and threw him to the ground and began to beat his face with my fist. I took the bat from him and hit him three times with the bat, and at that moment, I felt God pull me back. I might have killed him if the Lord had not stopped me. He later filed charges against me, but the D.A. dropped the case because he lied about what happened, and the evidence proved I acted in self-defense. I am ashamed about the whole ordeal that I didn't have better control of my emotions and paid a heavy price with my wife, which had every right to be outraged; however, she stuck by my side, and we got through it.

It turns out his wife was in the house the whole time and ran out screaming as we fought. Confused and puzzled, I asked her with a frustrated and angered voice, why didn't you tell him I never said you couldn't counsel with anyone else? She blurted out some nonsensical hysterical incoherent statement, but it was all a lie, the wolf was finally revealed. Smiling faces, pretend to be your friend, smiling faces show no traces of the evil that lurks within (can you dig it?)"

I regret not heeding to the voice of the Holy Spirit when He told me not to call the husband back, but we make mistakes, and prayerfully learn from them. No matter how bad the situation is, no matter how angry we get, even if you feel you have no way out, always seek to hear the Holy Spirit, He will lead you into all truth. Jesus says, ***My sheep know my voice, and a stranger's voice they will not follow-*** John 10:27. I followed a strange voice that evening, a voice not of God. Yes, it was self-defense, but if I had listened to the Holy Spirit I would not have had to defend myself, for He is my defender!

Chapter Thirteen

NOT MY WILL, BUT YOURS!

"In whom also we have obtained an inheritance, being predestined according to the purpose of him who worketh all things after the counsel of his own will:" (Ephesians 1:11).

"And all the inhabitants of the earth are reputed as nothing: and he doeth according to his will in the army of heaven, and among the inhabitants of the earth: and none can stay his hand, or say unto him, What doest thou?" (Daniel 4:35).

God's Permissive and Sovereign will:

Even though God is sovereign and has providence over our lives, such a view of God while encouraging should never lend the excuse not to take responsibility for our actions and decisions. We are all responsible and will give an account before the Great Throne of God (Romans 14:12).

So, if God is sovereign and providential, where does free will have its place? Why would it make a difference what we do if God has already pre-ordained, pre-purposed, pre-chosen, and pre-selected every second of our existence? In our finite mind, it just doesn't add up; it doesn't make sense; it is unfathomable to comprehend and to some degree, we think, not fair. But God is infinite in all that He is and does, *His thoughts are not our thoughts, His ways are not our ways:* He is God! And we are not; and some things aren't our business!

How can everything take place according to His will when our will often runs contrary to His? Theologians try to pin this question with a thought called the "Hidden Will and the Revealed Will of God." God's hidden will are those things that cannot be known to man, it is beyond man's understanding, and he is unable to calculate the Universe in its total sum of moveable parts, dimensions and anomalies. Only God can direct or have a directive that will come to pass because He directs everything. The fact that you and I can't even direct tomorrow accurately should put in perspective the AWE-someness of God, for He has done it for an eternity. However, God has allowed us to play a role within His Universal decree of providence; He has given us enough information about ourselves, this world and Himself that man can plot a course of action based on limited knowledge that will affect his way of life by each action and decision we make. For the child of God, our will should be gleaned from the gold nuggets of God's Word. The Word is like the Yellow Brick Road that leads to the most powerful being in existence, but unlike the Wizard of Oz God is not a phony. He is not a little man pretending to be big and all-powerful all-knowing and all-seeing; God really is those things. We can know God's will through His Word, which is His Son Jesus Christ, *"for in these last days He speaks to us through His Son." Hebrews 1:2.* Christ has been revealed to us plainly, but the hidden or "secret things" belong to the LORD our God, but the things that are shown belong to our children and to us forever." (Deut. 29:29).

[19]In his article in Table Talk Magazine, "God's Control and Our Responsibility" DR. Guy M. Richard gives us another distinction, he writes *"When we refer to God as the primary or ultimate cause of all things, we are simply acknowledging that God is sovereign and that He acts sovereignly. We are saying that nothing catches Him by surprise, that nothing*

[19] Guy M. Richard, PhD., *God's Control And Our Responsibility*, Table Talk Magazine, page 9, October 2018, February 2020

happens by accident, that there is no "maverick molecule" or maverick force in the universe that is outside of God's power and control, and that everything that happens is part of God's decretive will. But although God is the primary or ultimate cause of everything that happens, He is not the only cause."

You can run, but you can't hide from God:

If you will allow me to summarize about the prophet Jonah to make Dr. Richards point.

God commands Jonah to go to the city of Nineveh to prophesy against it, "for their great wickedness is come up before Me," the LORD says, but Jonah instead attempts to flee from "the presence of the LORD" by going to Jaffa, and sailing to Tarshish, a city in the opposite direction. A massive storm arises and the sailors, realizing that it is no ordinary storm cast lots and discover that Jonah is to blame. Jonah admits he is the reason and if they were to throw him overboard the storm would cease. The sailors refused to do this and continue rowing, but all their efforts failed, and they were eventually forced to throw Jonah overboard. As a result, the storm calms and the sailors then offer sacrifices to God. Jonah is miraculously saved by being swallowed by a large fish in whose belly he spends three days and three nights. While in the great fish Jonah prays to God in his affliction and commits to thanking God and to pay what he has vowed. God then commands the fish to vomit Jonah out.

God always gets what He wants. There are incalculable ways God can orchestrate His will; He has all the elements of the universe at His disposal, all created beings are as putty in His hands, and He has all the time in the world to accomplish His purpose. God can redeem the time to work out the time we have wasted. The hilarious thing about Jonah's attempt to flee from God and run the opposite direction is, it is believed, the enormous fish vomited Jonah out at the same place God first commanded Jonah. I can see that; God usually brings you back to the place you disobey Him. In reality, our call is about what God wants to do through us. The apostle Paul says *"I am crucified with Christ; and it is no longer I who live, but it is Christ who lives in me."—Galatians 2:20*

God is not swayed by our attempts to escape or our emotional outbursts. Jonah had a legitimate reason not to go to Nineveh, they had persecuted Jonah's people, committed horrible crimes against them. However, God commands us to forgive. I believe this charge to Jonah from God was for him as well as salvation for the people of Nineveh. Though Jonah had a will, it could not supplant God's ultimate will.

Our past experience often influences our present will. I know people, parishioners, friends, and spouses can hurt us, and we have a right to be angry but you have a command to forgive. When we run from our call or quit our assignment because of people's attempts to derail us or say things to upset us or do something that unsettles us, then, what God has proposed for others through us may be altered negatively. We can create storms for people we love when we run from God. The sailors had to throw Jonah overboard because of Jonah's disobedience, which caused Jonah unnecessary grief and the crewmen's potential demise. When we let our past hurts interfere with God's present work in us, it can have an impact on your purpose and on others who need a message from God. Don't run from God; No one wants to be in the belly of a fish for three days and nights. That had to be disgusting!

Before the foundation of the world, God called you. It is not in your power to fulfill your heavenly Father's calling in your life; it is in the Father's grace that we meet our calling. I'm sure the Apostle Paul wanted to quit many times. He wanted the thorn in his flesh to be taken away, but God said, *"My grace is sufficient."* Yes, we have free will, but God's eternal and effectual calling supersedes our will. God can compose His will as a brilliant conductor does a complex symphony to interact with our own instrument of the will and still get an artistic masterpiece, with or without us; though He prefers with us. In His eternal purpose God is not limited, He cannot be thwarted by our feeble attempt to disobey Him. God allows our free will and choice to be in play up to a point, but think not if God wants it, He can't get it. So, if you are really called, rest assured, I believe you will complete your purpose no matter how dire the circumstances. God has equipped us to endure, overcome, and conquer. *No weapon, formed against you, can prosper;* it's impossible. Since no weapon can prosper against you, what reason or excuse can we use not to continue in ministry, in marriage, or any other thing for the kingdom of God and His righteousness.

The Apostle Paul writes in (Colossians 3:22) *"Bondservants, obey in all things your masters according to the flesh, not with eyeservice, as men-pleasers, but in sincerity of heart, fearing God. And whatever you do, do it heartily, as to the Lord and not men, knowing that from the Lord you will receive the reward of your inheritance; for you serve the Lord."*

The word Bondservant means slave, literal or figurative, involuntary or voluntary; a sense of subjection, a (bondman), servant. Paul's view is clear, whatever we are called to do, particularly for the Lord, we are to do it wholeheartedly and with sincerity of heart. When God calls us, we are not our own; we belong to Him; *we have been bought with a price* to fulfill the work of ministry. *"For we are His workmanship, created in Christ Jesus for good works, which God prepared beforehand that we should walk in them."* (Ephesians 2:10).

Practically, how do you know God called you?

You must aspire to do the work of ministry. You may or may not have the aspiration to be a pastor or preach before you are called. For some, God must pull and tug until they surrender to the call. But once you surrender, there isn't anything else you want more than to serve God, in whatever capacity He calls you. I know! God had to pull and tug me for a few years before I surrendered, but once I did my desire to serve His people became my aspiration.

[20]Martyn Lloyd-Jones said, in his sermon *The Preacher* at a Pastors' Conference: "If there is anything else a man can do other than preach, he ought to do it. The pulpit is no place for him". Preaching and pastoring is not merely something an individual can do, but what he must do. He is called and compelled by a Force that lays upon him this desire, this compulsion to enter the pulpit. This called-man, Lloyd-Jones writes, would rather die than live without preaching. Likewise, the legendary pastor Charles H. Spurgeon says: "If you can do anything else, do it. If you can stay out of the ministry, stay out of the ministry."

What are these icons of preaching saying? I believe they are saying a preacher and the pastor must be called by God. It's not just a vocation but a life; it's what you are. If you were born male, it's what you are; if you were born Asian, it's who you are. If you were born again to be a preacher or pastor, it's who you were born again to be.

In other words, only those who believe they are chosen by God for the pulpit should proceed in undertaking this sacred task. "Preachers are born, not made, You will never teach a man to be a preacher if he is not already one."

But aspiration in and of itself does not mean you are called. There must be an *affirmation*, and a confirmation you are called by God. Affirmation is, most often, people affirming your spiritual gifts. They see the "Spiritual Gift" of preaching, pastoring and teaching, etc. on your life. If no one is confirming you're a good teacher you are not called to pastor God's people. One of the most important gifts for the pastor is to teach, to feed the flock of Christ.

When Jesus asked Peter, "Peter, do you love Me," Peter replied, ``Lord, you know I do." Jesus then says, "Feed my sheep." The pastor must be able to feed God's people God's Word. This is the only way sheep grow up to maturity; pretty and polite preaching may tickle the

---

[20] Martin Lloyd-Jones, *The Preacher,* Pastor's Conference, April 13 2007, February 2020

ears of the hearers, but without substantive teaching, they will remain malnourished and soon die off, both spiritually and numerically.

Lloyd-Jones stated, as it pertains to the call:

First, the "*inner compulsion*"- I take this to mean, there is a duress within the soul, as if the soul is compelled to such a degree it cannot resist the necessity, the yearning is too strong, it powers too persuasive not just to do it, but to become it.

Second, an "*outside influence*" meaning, this will be connected with the call. Your gift will make room for you. In other words, people will begin to see this anointing in your life. Opportunities will start to open for you to speak before people in the church or in the pulpit. Space must be made for your gift, you don't have to force your gift into space God creates a space for you. Generally, your pastor will notice your gift and acknowledge it. Also, spiritually mature Christians will see this gift in you, for they know the Spirit by the Spirit. They will often encourage you to hear and seek God for confirmation in your call.

Third, one called will experience a "*loving concern* for others." You will begin to love those that hate you. You will love them, and there's nothing they can do about it. God gives His preachers and pastors a heart like His. A new awareness of the lost becomes a condition of the heart. A new light within you is waiting to expose darkness, and it must shine on the road of salvation for others to see. You want to see the lost saved from the gates of hell and placed in the gates of heaven, and this light compels you to share it.

Fourth, there is an "*overwhelming constraint*" within the one called to do this work. Lloyd-Jones maintained there will be "a sense of constraint,". I get the image of a straitjacket, something that confines the preacher to preach, though he may want to do something else, his straitjacket won't allow him.

He must preach in season and out of season. He must preach the truth, not words that tickle the ears of the listeners. No matter the cost, he must preach! Lloyd-Jones recognizes this when he states: "*You do your utmost to push back and to rid yourself of this disturbance in your spirit which comes in these various ways. But you reach the point when you cannot do so any longer. It almost becomes an obsession, and so overwhelming that in the end you say, "I can do nothing else, I cannot resist any longer."*

Fifth, the man who is called to preach comes under a "*sobering humility*." He must *trust in the LORD with all his heart and lean not to his own understanding*. He has a keen sense he is not worthy of this holy calling. He must postulate his heart as the apostle Paul, *"For I am the least of the apostles, and not fit to be called an apostle, because I persecuted the church of God."* 1 Corithians 15:9. The God-called man knows he is not fit, he is not worthy; he is astutely aware of his own sin and ashamed of it. He knows his righteousness is as filthy rags. He is in awe of the holiness of God and trembles at the task which he has been assigned, and yet, he is drawn like a moth to the flame. Lloyd-Jones writes, "The man who is called by God is a man who realizes what he is called to do, and he so realizes the awfulness of the task that he shrinks from it."

Sixth, "A *corporate confirmation"* is necessary to the one called to preach. He asserts, there should be a formal commissioning of the church to send the preacher but must be proven and examined before the preacher is sent. Using (Romans 10:13-15) as an example this is an essential part of the call. Hands must be laid upon him in recognition of what God is doing in his life. These are the requirements Lloyd-Jones believed to the mark of one truly called.

In addition, I believe there is a **seventh** distinguishing mark that Lloyd-Jones touches on, but I would like to dig a little deeper. A person called to the preaching ministry must have a "*divine confirmation*." This preoccupation is pulled from outside the natural. It is directed from the spiritual realm and comes with Spiritual persuasion and powers to prompt a man to preach. He can't hide for long; he can't wash his hands of it, he is unable to withstand the long barrage of weight if he flees from the call, it becomes too heavy. Then he is left to the gift of faith. As a quadriplegic who has been given a cure gets out of his wheelchair with the hope that the treatment will work, the preacher puts one foot in front of the other until faith secures him in his calling.This divine calling, grips the soul and governs the spirit. It becomes an overwhelming obsession that cannot be discarded. It will not go away nor leave a man to himself, there is no way to escape. Such a strong force lays hold of the man that he is held captive. It is the definitive seal of one's calling. Without a divine calling, I believe, no one should shepherd the Lord's sheep.

What do I mean by "Divine"? An irrefutable event that takes place in your life that only God can bring about to confirm your call.

For instance, when running from my call to preach I still had opportunities to teach Bible study, lead the men's ministry and so on. Often, people would say after a class how much they enjoyed my teaching. Soon, after teaching for a while people would ask me, "When will you pastor a church?" Or, suggested I should become a pastor. That is what I consider the affirmation part of the calling. As God's hand weighed heavier on me to preach and pastor His church, He made it clear in my mind and heart through signs and wonders that only God could orchestrate, which is a divine confirmation, and each person experiences this confirmation in their own way which I will discuss later with a personal testimony. In the final analysis, it is God, not man-and God, not self that gives the call but God alone according to (Ephesians 4:11-12) *"And He Himself gave some to be apostles, some prophets, some evangelists, and some- pastors and teacher, for the equipping of the saints for the work of ministry, for the edifying of the body of Christ."*

"He Himself gave gifts," it is Jesus that calls us into ministry, not we ourselves. Do you feel called to ministry? Is there a stirring inside you?

Chapter Fourteen

THEOLOGY-LITE SERMONS

"Preach the word; be instant in season, out of season; reprove, rebuke, exhort with all longsuffering and doctrine." (2 Timothy 4:2)

If you are called to preach, preach the whole gospel, PLEASE! Every Sunday, you will find preachers and pastors preaching the "Good News." Our sermons are full of inspiration, motivation, and hope. Many preach the gospel, the cross, and redemption; some attempt to preach suffering, sin, and hell, albeit the watered-down version or what I call "theology light" sermons. Many preach the "good news" is prosperity, grace, victory, live your best life now, etc.... all of those things are true to some extent and it certainly fills the seats. But what about the other part of the gospel? You know, the part that says we must suffer for the gospel's sake, (1 Peter 2:21). *"For to this you were called, because Christ also suffered for us, leaving us an example, that you should follow His steps."*

Or what about (1 Peter 4: 1-6), *Therefore, since Christ suffered in his body, arm yourselves also with the same attitude, because he who has suffered in his body is done with sin. As a result, he does not live the rest of his earthly life for evil human desires, but rather for the will of God. For you have spent enough time in the past doing what pagans choose to do—living in debauchery, lust, drunkenness, orgies, carousing and detestable idolatry. They think it is strange that you do not plunge with them into the same flood of dissipation,* ***and they heap abuse on you.*** *But they will have to give account to him who is ready to judge the living and the dead."*

When the lost, the unbelievers and the unregenerate see two tales of one story they are more often left confused than converted. What do I mean? If we are only preaching grace and prosperity and no suffering, we paint a confusing picture to the world; because some of God's people are suffering at different times of their life. All true believers will suffer at one time or another for the gospel's sake; it is unavoidable. Suffering is not a bad thing, it is a tool by which God uses to correct us and grow us spiritually and to show the power of His grace:

"Of course, you get no credit for being patient if you are beaten for doing wrong. But if you suffer for doing good and endure it patiently, God is pleased with you" (1 Peter 2:20) NLT.

When we only preach prosperity, what happens to "*the poor will be with you always?*" Do they not have a place at the Lord's table? Don't get me wrong, all I'm saying is preach both; the whole gospel, Jesus did, Paul certainly did and so should we as preachers and pastors. The world needs preaching that will convict the heart not just make the heart warm and fuzzy.

People need to be saved from hell, not possess more stuff, and sometimes we must preach to preach the hell out of them. The Lord Jesus has entrusted us to preach His gospel, not our version of it. Therefore, the saved, the redeemed ought to know that both heaven and hell are at play, righteousness and wickedness are ever before us, light and darkness are the two isles before us and holiness and sin are warring inside us. This is one tale of two cities, the kingdom of God and the kingdom of Satan, the flesh and the spirit.

Are we to preach victory without the battle, success without failure, the crown without the cross, material gain without internal change? Do we dismiss holy living and holy behavior? Are we to circumvent God's commandment because of grace, the apostle Paul says, "God forbid!" certainly not; Jesus says, *"If you love Me keep My commandments."* As Christians, we are no longer under the law of sin and death but we are under the law of Christ; and He said to the woman caught in adultery after He extended her grace, *"God. and sin no more".* His grace does not give us the liberty to sin.

Paul say's *"Now the works of the flesh are evident, which are: adultery, fornication, uncleanness, lewdness,* [20] *idolatry, sorcery, hatred, contentions, jealousies, outbursts of wrath, selfish ambitions, dissensions, heresies,* [21] *envy, murders, drunkenness, revelries, and the like; of which I tell you beforehand, just as I also told you in time past, that those* ***who practice*** *such things* ***will not*** *inherit the kingdom of God."* (Galatians 5:19-21)

It's one thing to fall, stumble and fumble, but to ***practice*** sin means living in it and improving upon it. I am reminded of my High School football days; we would spend hours in the hot summer sun in "Two-a-days" practice to get better at our skillset and position. The heat in Texas in the middle of August should be criminal and yet, the team would endure the heat because we all wanted to play. That is what practicing sin is like; you will endure all kinds of suffering to play in the game of fleshly desire. The more sin you crave, the more you practice getting it; (James 1:14,15) *"But each one is tempted when he is drawn away by his own desires and enticed. Then, when desire is conceived, it gives birth to sin, and sin, when it is full-grown, brings forth death."*

Those who practice such things "WILL NOT" inherit the kingdom of God. Pastors, preachers, and teachers, if we are avoiding these kinds of scriptures and text to keep the seats full, then we are aiding and abetting people to hell, and their blood is on our hands; and we will have seats filled with demons rather than disciples. On Judgement Day, God will not allow His preachers to hide behind LOVE as an excuse for not preaching the whole gospel.

The Apostle Paul says all he wants, *"Is to know Christ and Him crucified, and to know the power of His resurrection, and the fellowship of His suffering?"* Paul is preaching the whole gospel.

The more I study this great man of God; I'm convinced he loved Jesus and allowed himself to come before the Lord exposed in his full nakedness about his shortcomings and failures. The courage it took for this highly educated man with power and prestige to surrender his will to the will of Christ, and to humble himself, to humiliate himself before God and man is truly astounding. Within Paul's spirit he wrestles with two natures, *those things I want to do; I do not, and the things I don't want to do, I find myself doing them*. Romans 7:15-20.

This is the rawest form of honesty about one's self. This great spiritual man of God, one of only a handful that had the privilege of seeing heaven before he died, hearing and seeing things that could not even be repeated; this man that literally met Jesus on Damascus road, and was inspired to write three fourth of the New Testament, this man that raised people from the dead and healed the cripple, this man with all his earthly accolades, say's, "I COUNT THEM AS DUNG," and said, "*I will only boast in my suffering*." **Where's that church today?**

What a vast contrast to today's preachers. We want to boast in our victories, our accomplishments, our large church attendance, and exuberant lifestyle. Listen, I include myself in that statement. I love to talk about the abundant blessing of God but He has tempered my heart with the *balance* to preach the Word in season and out of season, popular or not. Paul did both, but the humility Paul exhibits the risk to be ridiculed by his followers and foes for his personal struggles is so refreshing and rewarding; it rests upon the soul like morning dew upon the grass. His message of suffering for righteousness, although difficult and often painful, softly lands upon the soul and eases the pain and embarrassment of the struggle and unbalance one goes through in life. Whether it be business failures, career disappointments, relationship issues, marriage problems, and yes, personal sin. We are all on the same journey, there is no struggle uncommon to man, there is nothing new under the sun. Even those born with a silver spoon must walk this road of trial and tribulation. Nor are the righteous exempt from afflictions, pain, sickness, and diseases.

Blameless, and still, I suffer? Remember Job? He said, *"Man is born, and his days are full of trouble."*

[6] "Now there was a day when the sons of God came to present themselves before the Lord, and Satan[b] also came among them. [7] The Lord said to

Satan, "From where have you come?" Satan answered the Lord and said, "From going to and fro on the earth, and from walking up and down on it."
[8] And the Lord said to Satan, "Have you considered my servant Job, that there is none like him on the earth, a blameless and upright man, who fears God and turns away from evil?"
[9] Then Satan answered the Lord and said, "Does Job fear God for no reason?
[10] Have you not put a hedge around him and his house and all that he has, on every side? You have blessed the work of his hands, and his possessions have increased in the land.
[11] But stretch out your hand and touch all that he has, and he will curse you to your face."
[12] And the Lord said to Satan, "Behold, all that he has is in your hand. Only against him do not stretch out your hand." So Satan went out from the presence of the Lord." Job 1:6-12.

You know the rest of the story, Satan killed his children, took all he owned and plagued Job with unbearable sickness.

[20] "Then Job arose and tore his robe and shaved his head and fell on the ground and worshiped.
[21] And he said, "Naked I came from my mother's womb, and naked shall I return. The Lord gave, and the Lord has taken away; blessed be the name of the Lord."
[22] In all this Job did not sin or charge God with wrong."

The point I'm making is, the righteousness of God in Christ Jesus will suffer for being righteous. It matters not how anointed you are or how large or small your church is or how famous or humble you are; if you're doing it for Christ, there will be suffering. It is Satan's mission to steal, kill, and destroy God's people, and guess what? God gives Satan a short arm to try, Even against His elect. The devil is God's devil, and God uses His devil sometimes to bring us to repentance, but it's all designed to award you with a greater anointing and faith.

The other day, I came across a video of Bishop T.D. Jake's giving an emotional testimony while preaching; I usually don't watch preachers on TV, but this episode caught my attention. He was talking about the struggles he has gone through to get where he is in ministry, as most of us know unless you're from Mars, he is one of the most popular preachers of our day. He exclaimed, and I'm paraphrasing; the success God has allowed him to have, the anointing God has placed upon on his life is not because of his dynamic preaching ability, or extensive vocabulary, or any other high-profile abilities he might have but because of all the pain and suffering he has had to endure. The pain of losing his mother-in-law and mother in a two-year span, which he says "was devastating to him, to the point he literally almost lost his mind. The anguish the suffering the torment he felt when he learned his 13 year old daughter was pregnant. All these situations were in the middle of his popularity. One of the things he said that I totally agree with is that you can't run with him and expect to have the same anointing he has until you have gone through what he has endured. This was not said in an arrogant or pompous way at all. He was simply stating, to get that kind of anointing you have to go through His kind of suffering and still be faithful.

You can't have the crown without the cross.

Paul, the apostle is basically saying the same thing, the greater the anointing the greater the suffering. Paul strips away all the standard and mundane religious lingo and fake posture behavior and shares with us the battle of pressing toward the mark, pushing through the suffering of ministry. And he suffered tremendously; all while battling with his own flesh (Romans 7:13-25; Philippians 3:8-14). The Apostle Paul knows with honesty, he has not attained it fully, he knows with humility, he hasn't reached the mark, he knows his best life is to come when Jesus returns. If Paul can be this honest this forthcoming about his Christian walk, what about us? Please, please don't misunderstand, with my whole heart I know and believe God can and will bless us beyond measure and we already have the victory, but on this side of glory, blessings run alongside sufferings. Our Christian walk is two kingdoms ruled by one King. Satan may be "prince of the power of the air," but Jesus is King of kings and Lord of lords. Satan is God's devil, and God uses the suffering the devil brings for His own purposes.

Chapter Fifteen

THE CREATIVE ORDER OF MAN AND WOMAN

"That man is a creature who needs order yet yearns for change is the creative contradiction at the heart of laws which structures his conformity and define his deviancy." -Freda Adler

"Let all things be done decently and in order" (1 Corinthians 14;40)

Ordered by His Steps: See (Genesis 2:18-25)

Everything God does, He does by order and in order. The entire universe and everything in it are *ordered* and in order. Order is balance; disorder causes imbalance.

Example: God is the only One that can take dust from the ground, blow in it, and it doesn't scatter or blow away in the wind, but bring order and life to a living soul. Without order, life is dust blown away in the wind. Only the LORD God is capable of designing an incalculable, immeasurable, indeterminable universe; yet, hold the answer in Himself to its immensity of calculations and order. Only the All-Knowing, the All-Present, and the All-Powerful can set limits and order to what is not seen nor fully understood. Even when it seems chaotic, it is through God's sovereignty this universe exists and is balanced. The earth sets on its axis and so does the Universe, but only

God knows where it is and what it is. Remember when God reprimands and sends Job's head spinning (Job 38:3-6):

"Now prepare yourself like a man; I will question you, and you shall answer Me. Where were you when I laid the foundations of the earth? Tell Me, if you have understanding. Who determined its measurement? Surely you know! Or who stretched the line upon it? To what were its foundations fastened? Or who laid its cornerstone", and in verse 33 it continues, *Knowest thou the ordinance of heaven? KJV*

Just in these few verses we are privy to and allowed to see vaguely behind the scene of creation. The LORD God does not go so far as to give us the answer, but He makes it plain and clear He is supremely omniscient, omnipotent, omnipresent and in control of all things. When God created man and woman He established an order by which they would live, and a gender role they would possess. In the Garden of Eden, the **law of God is complete** and perfect. However, sin entered the world, and a *new world* order was ushered in.

Though this present world seems disordered and frenzied, it is in order on two fronts. (Eph. 2:2,3) shows a world order:

"Wherein in time past ye walked according to the course of this world, according to the prince of the power of the air, the spirit that now worketh in the children of disobedience; among whom also we all had our conversation in times past in the lust of our flesh and of the mind; and were by nature the children of wrath, even as others." KJV

First, we can see, this present world is ruled by Satan and ordered the way he wants it. Second, we know God supersedes all rulers and kingdoms and will soon set all things under Christ's feet. *Every knee shall bow and every tongue shall confess that Jesus Christ, King of kings and Lord of lords will have restored dominion over all things once again.*

Only God knows all the variables, and incalculable ways things can go wrong, and the inconceivable and unimaginable forces that push against His creative order and marriage institution. Therefore, He has reordered His vast plan of redemption through His Son by way of personal experience and application of the gospel to live according to His word. Because we cannot see all that God sees we must learn to trust Him and walk by faith in our marriage. Most of us married without any Biblical knowledge of what marriage is; each partner brought their hidden suitcase full of issues and began to unpack it in the marriage. This suitcase was hidden under the bed while you were dating or living together. In most premarital relationships our entire bag of issues are not fully unpacked. We may be aware of some of the character flaws, but not all. This is why, early on in the marriage it is a mystery why we didn't know specific weaknesses about your mate while dating or shacking. When couples live together before they are married, there isn't any real commitment, and in most cases we reserve all of who we are in fear of losing the one we think we will spend the rest of our lives. We don't want to expose all the embarrassing things that are in the suitcase. But "shacking" causes a cloaked disorder in the relationship, the joining may appear to be in order because the flesh is being pacified and pleased but your spirit is displeased.

(Ephesians 5:21,32) [31]"***For this cause shall a man leave his father and mother, and shall be joined unto his wife, and they two shall be one flesh.***[32] ***This is a great mystery: but I speak concerning Christ and the church".***

When God created Eve, she was the FATHER's daughter. It was God that brought Eve to Adam, not to cohabitate or live together, but to marry. Shacking up.... or however you prefer to coin it, will never have the teeth, the bite, the binding that a Christ centered marriage has. There is no covenant without marriage, no real obligation, which we will discuss in the next chapter.

Without understanding the husband and wife's order, we will have a disorder in our marriage. Order is not a negative connotation but a positive one. Order is stability; it brings about a calm, harmonious, and symmetry to that which is **in** order.

Order casts out confusion, it eliminates distraction, it binds misperception and misunderstanding. It alleviates out of controlled emotions and it produces faith, hope, and confidence in the person that is in order- because the LORD orders their steps.

Your image is what you imagine it to be: This would seem easy and logical, and in reality, it is; but something has ***clogged*** the flow of the godly image of man and woman in marriage. It is as though a thick fog has swooped in unawares and made the plain words of God hard to see. It appears that just about every marriage is disoriented in this hellish fog. We have all heard the statistics on marriage which is alarming in and of itself, but what we should be alarmed about is the statistics of how many Christians are not applying God's created order and correct image of themselves in their marriages. This has nothing to do with statistics, political correctness, current cultural trends or acceptance, feelings, or emotions, or how we are born, but God's word has determined what our image is to be.

Being still in hearing and obeying God's word is a matter of the heart. Have you conditioned your new heart to receive new instructions? *New wine won't fit in an old wineskin! Mark 2:22.* What do I mean? Your old image of how you saw yourself cannot fit into the new image God has given you today. You have been born again! Born with the original image–the image of Christ, which is the exact replica and the expressed image of God. This is the image Adam and Eve had before the Fall. *Old things have passed away, behold, all things are made new.*

We must learn to identify with our new righteous nature, not our old sinful nature; we must set our minds on those things above, not those things below. In the original order of Man and Woman in marriage, we must see it as it was designed in heaven to be manifest on earth.

Men and women, husbands, and wives do not have a marriage problem; they have an image problem. How we see ourselves is how we present ourselves; we can hide this image for a time and give a false representation, but sooner or later, the real picture about you will present you. You can't escape you for long; "you" must be put on display. You have the ability to choose and display what and who you believe you are; the old John or the new John? When you look in the mirror, do you see Alicia or the Christ in Alicia? When God looks at you, He first sees His Son in you; this was God's plan from the beginning, to see Himself in you, which is why you were created in His image.

"7 For a man indeed ought not to cover his head, since he is the image and glory of God; but woman is the glory of man. 8 For man is not from woman, but woman from man. 9 Nor was man created for the woman, but woman for the man. 10 For this reason the woman ought to have a symbol of authority on her head, because of the angels. (1 Corinthians 11:9)

Let's start with the elephant in the room: I can understand, at first reading, without the right perspective of the lens, this verse could cause uneasiness in women. At first glance the apostle may sound a little sexist, old fashioned, and out of touch with today's woman. But these are not the words of Paul, these are the words of the Holy Spirit who has inspired the apostle to write them. We must not view this text through the lens of our own understanding, but through the eyes of God, and His sovereign purpose.

Men often neglect the next part of the scripture: ***11 Nevertheless, neither is man independent of woman, nor woman independent of man, in the Lord. 12 For as woman came from man, even so man also comes through woman; but all things are from God."***

Once God created Eve from Adam, man's only entrance into this world is through a woman. She is the mother of all living. How awesome is God! He knows Eve was deceived and led her husband to sin, but God is so merciful that He blessed the woman to birth the man Jesus, who would lead man back to righteousness and fellowship with God. Through woman, man was led into transgression, likewise, man is led to redemption through her Son Jesus.

After the Fall, Adam and Eve had the wrong image of themselves. Think about it; when God came walking in the cool of the day. He asked Adam, "Where are you?" Adam was not the same person; his image was changed; that's why he hid. He no longer knew himself and he was ashamed. His nakedness never bothered him before, until his eyes were open, meaning, he saw himself as dirt no longer fully endowed with the image of God. As I stated earlier, what you imagine your image to be is what you will present. I believe this is why the unsaved, the unregenerate behave as they do, they see themselves as only human; but God never calls us human He calls us Mankind made in the image of Him. Mankind is the name God gave His image on earth. God was not asking Adam about proximity when He said, "Where are you;" God was asking Adam, where has My image gone?

In one sense, God knew this new fallen distorted image would cause a battle between the sexes; and in the other, He made sure they would have to depend on each other; they are interdependent of each other.

In (Genesis 1:26-31), Man is given dominion over the fish of the sea, the birds of the sky, the cattle and over all the earth, over every creeping thing that creeps on the earth. He is decreed to be fruitful and multiply and fill the earth. Adam could not do this unless he had a companion. At this point in the sixth-day creation he is still incomplete; by this, I mean deficient in his purpose. He was complete as a man, but he was not finished as Mankind. Mankind included the *Woman*. He needs a partner; he needs an equal, a helper to compliment him in fulfilling the task of having dominion over the earth.

All the animals are male and female, but not so with Adam; inevitably, this would cause a feeling of loneliness in him. *It was not good for man to be alone*. So, to complete man and fulfill his purpose, God needed to create a woman. Not as an afterthought, but a planned ordered purpose. Eve was his help-meet to fulfill God's order for mankind.

This word ***helpmeet*** is an interesting word. In Hebrew, it is Ezer-kenegdo. And it means a helper like him or corresponding to him or face to face with him. Somebody who is a perfect fit for man to make him capable of reproduction and ruling. Let's look again at 1 Corinthians 11:7. *"Man is the image and glory of God, but the woman is the glory of man."*

[21]John MacArthur writes, ***"The woman is the glory of man. Man is the reflection of the glory of God. Man is uniquely created to bear the image of God as a ruler who is given a spear of sovereignty. In that sense he is created to be the glory of God. God is the sovereign ruler and man is created and given dominion to be sovereign ruler over all the created world, to care for the creation according to God's divine plan." Man was given rulership of the world. It is true, "both men and women are created in God's image," Genesis 1:27 says that. But it is man who is created from the dust of the ground and it is woman who is created from the side of man."***

Since the Fall, has that order changed? I don't think so. Though perverted and spoiled by sin, God's original plan is still in order but now compromised according to (Genesis 3:16) ***Your desire shall be for your husband God says to the woman and he shall rule over you.***

In one sense, McArthur is correct, but also in (Genesis 1:26), it says, *"let* ***them*** *have dominion."* Is God still referring to just the male and not the female? Or is God including women in that decree? I believe as it pertains to marriage this does include the wife. Note as it continues in (v27,28) *"So God created man in His own image; in the image of God He created him; male and female He created* ***them****. Then God blessed* ***them****, and God said to* ***them****, ''Be fruitful and multiply; fill the earth and subdue it; have dominion over the fish of the sea, over the birds of the air, and over every living thing moves on the earth."*

As it pertains to male and female, men will always have natural authority over women, it is an order set by God. But as it relates to the marriage institution, I believe this authority is shared. However, man is the head of that authority but the woman is the balance of

[21] John McArthur, *The Creation of Woman Sermons*, November 28, 1999, February 2020

that authority. Marriage brings balance to the creative order of mankind, and the wife radiates power with her husband, but should never hijack or confiscate her husbands' authority. When men try and usurp Christ's headship over their lives man's authority becomes illegitimate and corrupt; so too, it is prudent for the woman not to enlist her husband's headship; this happened in the Garden! When Eve took the head position of authority to speak to the serpent, she usurped Adam's authority. Why Adam let that happen, I'll deal with that later!

The woman is created to help man. Help man do what? Yes, in procreation, having dominion over the earth, reflecting the image of God, and being God's governors on earth together. But I believe God created Eve for another purpose also, to help man fight the enemy that would surely come, which is the serpent, that old devil. The word ***helpmeet***, "ezreconegdo"- *Ezre-* is used multiple times in the Bible to assist someone in need of help or hardship, or about to go to war. It is even used to submit God's help, "for the LORD will be your help." ***Conegdo- to stand across, face to face, comparable, or equal.***

Certainly, God knew Satan would trick Eve, but I think it is also plausible God created Eve to help Adam against the guile of the serpent but fell prey to it herself? Perhaps Eve became overzealous to help her husband and thought she could protect him from the snake, but it was not her place to protect but to help; **to come to aid in defense, to unify the front against attack. To be a reinforcement in hardship and distress; by encouraging her husband not to give in to the temptation to come.** It is a wise woman who knows how to help her husband without letting the husband know he is being helped.

However, we know the story, because Eve tried to banter with the serpent by herself, she was deceived, and instead of standing with her husband within ***their*** headship of authority, she usurped it and fell to deception.

Perhaps, Satan pursued Eve because she was Adam's reinforcement. If the devil solicited Adam first, he knew Eve would come to encourage him to resist, to *"help"* him to fight the temptation to keep him grounded in God's word. Surely, Adam loved Eve and would hear her words over the serpents. Satan knew Eve was the key to his success. He knew she would do anything to protect her husband, so he deceived her as if he wanted to help her and her husband become like God. He took advantage of what God created in her to be. In one sense she usruped her husband's authority, but in the other, I think Eve loved Adam so much she instinctively wanted to put him as a god in her life, possibly even above Elohim/God. Why do I say that, because if she wanted to usurp Adam's authority, she would have never shared the fruit with him but use it as a means of *knowledge of good and evil* giving her the seemingly upper hand over him?

Wives, you can't fight the battle for your husband, but you are equipped by God to help him in the fight.

The glory of God and the splendor of man:

God created man out of the dirt and made him reflect God's glory, as a diamond out of the earth would reflect its radiance and beauty, but the woman was created to perfect the iridescence of her husband. Eve gave Adam ***iridescence***. Iridescence is the amount of beauty, luminosity, radiance and splendor that emanates from a diamond. Adam was God's image, but not all of God's iridescent glory. Eve was the other part of God's image and when God created her to come face to face with her husband, and become one flesh with him, the iridescences of God reached its full splendor, brilliance, grandeur, it's full earthly glory.

MacArthur states: ***"As far as saving grace goes, as far as sanctifying grace goes, a woman comes as deeply in the communion with God as a man. She is made equally in the image of God and that image is equally restored through faith in Jesus Christ. She is as much capable of being like Jesus as any man is capable of it."***

Everything God gave Adam He gave Eve in terms of characteristics. Eve was perfect beauty and suited for Adam! She didn't need the help, the man did. I once heard Dr. Virginia Desmuke say, as she was teaching the women in the congregation, "Would you rather be the one giving the help, or the one that needs the help?" as all the men in the group quickly submerged into their egos.

What a beautiful picture (Genesis 2:18-25) paints; after Adam wakes up from his surgery, and God brings Eve to him for the first time, the first thing He says, *"This is bone of my bone; flesh of my flesh; she shall be called woman;"* Man, it must have been euphoric, nothing on earth was compatible to him until now. Nothing on earth was as beautiful as Eve, he was no longer alone in paradise and had a wife to share it. It's as though God was telling Adam, "This is what I took out of you, perfection, beauty, wisdom, and love; now I'm bringing her to you to help you be all I've created you to be."

God is so awesome, and He knows what He is doing. There is no reason for either sex to be envious, intimidated, or competitive. We were created to complement each other, and because we refuse to walk in our creative order and our new image, we allow the serpent to divide us over silly things, let alone major things. If we look at our original order through God's eyes, we can be fulfilled and complete in our roles.

There is another scenario why Eve took of the fruit. Satan's temptation wasn't the fruit itself but the questioning of God's law, and enticing Eve with the fruit of *individuality.* Eve, at first, simply saw fruit pleasant to the eyes and desirable to make her wise, but wiser than God wanted her to be, *"knowing good and evil."* We were never designed to know evil.

Satan saw division on the tree, an opportunity to divide the Creator from His creation. Satan is well acquainted with the Law of God; he broke it and was separated from God, cast down like lightning to the earth and separated one third of the angels from their Creator. Now He wants to separate God from man and the husband from his wife. Because man is created in the image of God, Satan hated man. Man remanded Satan of all of God's goodness, love, and perfection. Lucifer has fallen, he is no longer perfect, quite the opposite in fact. Lucifer caused division in heaven and he has caused it to be on earth.

God would later counter Satan's move with His "Son's body on the tree" to fulfill the law and unify His family once again. It was at the tree by which man fell and it was at the tree man was resurrected. It was the tree by which man lost his godly image and it was by the tree, through Christ crucifixion man received it again. Therefore, Jesus is unlike the forbidden fruit; whereas the fruit on the tree in the Garden brought death, Jesus, the first fruit of those who have died, was crucified on the tree (the Cross), brings life and reconciliation and unity.

Notice, Satan said, *'**You** shall not eat of every tree in the garden?' **You** is the second-person personal pronoun, in this case, referring to she, "Eve."* Satan is trying to create two from what God made ONE. He wants to build in Eve's mind she doesn't need man, or as some ladies like to say, "I can do bad all by myself." What destroys marriages more than anything else is individualism, thinking we can do it all by ourselves.

**__Individualism__- "the quality of being different from other people and doing things in your own way: the belief that individual people in society should have the right to make their own decisions, etc., rather than be controlled by the government" Oxford Dictionary*

"The moral stance, political philosophy, or social outlook that promotes independence and self-reliance of individual people, while opposing the interference with each person's choices by society, the state, or any other group or institution." -Definition Net

Individualism is a spirit, a spirit of independence. This evil spirit tries to cast this belief system into every person's heart, to divide husband from wife, man from woman, friends from each other, country, nations, churches from other churches, and most of all mankind from God. ***Individualism*** is divide and conquer. We were not created to be independent but interdependent.

Michael Jordan is known for a selfish quote, but holds weight, at his acceptance speech into the NBA Hall of Fame: "There is no "I" in team, but there is in win." But in the marriage team, there cannot be I in win; it must be ***we*** to win.

Moreover, my issue is not with Eve, yes, she's responsible for her disobedience to God, but mine is with Adam. I'm sure he meant well, but he dropped the ball on this one. The buck always stops at the head. He didn't protect and cover his wife the way Christ covers and protects His bride, the church. I speak on this in the next chapter

Chapter Sixteen

The Covenant of Marriage

"Everyone has a covenant and a purpose which is special, and if you do not fulfill it, there is no one else who will." -Glenda Green

21 *And the Lord God caused a deep sleep to fall on Adam, and he*
slept; and He took one of his ribs, and closed up the flesh in its place.
22 *Then the rib which the Lord God had taken from man He [b]*
made into a woman, and He brought her to the man. **23** *And Adam*
said: "This is now bone of my bones And flesh of my flesh; She shall
be called [c]Woman, Because she was taken out of [d]Man." **24**
Therefore a man shall leave his father and mother and be[e] joined to
his wife, and they shall become one flesh. Genesis 2:21-24

Why didn't God create the Woman independently? Surely, He could have, He had plenty of material to do so. I believe God wanted His creation to know what a covenant would mean. Spiritually speaking, God created man from God's heart. And just as He brought forth man from His heart, He brings forth woman from the rib which protects and is adjacent to the man's heart. She could not be created from Adams' heart because that belongs to God but she was designed from the closest thing to the heart, the rib. Man is to love the woman as the closest thing to his heart. Nothing is above her except God Himself. God made a covenant with Adam when God said He would make Adam a helpmeet. *"It is not good for man to be alone,"* Eve is God's covenant He would never leave Adam alone. ***The woman has the distinct honor of being God's reminder to all of mankind He would not leave us alone***, that God would become one with His creation. As stated earlier, though woman came out of man all of mankind would come out of her; it seems to me she has the grander privilege; there is no mankind without the woman.

In the kingdom of Heaven covenant means to become one flesh. In the eyes of God a covenant means to be inseparable, to be fused in such a way that to break the covenant would be to tear oneself apart. It was sin that tore man from God, but because of God's covenant with man He was determined to restore the covenant. When God made a covenant with Abraham God fitly joined Himself to Abraham, they, in a sense, became one flesh and no matter the circumstance, no matter the fault or feebleness of Abraham, no matter Israel's betrayal of God over the years, God would not, could not separate Himself from Israel because of the covenant.

Getting married is the biggest journey of life. Finding the right person, growing with them and then deciding that she/he is the one you want to be with for the rest of your life is an audacious commitment. When it comes time to pledge your affection and dedication to your spouse, the words you chose should not be taken lightly. Scripture says, *"It is better not to vow than to vow and not keep it."* *(Eccl 5:5)*

When you said, *"I promise to love, honor, and keep you, forsaking all others, as a faithful husband or wife as long as we both shall live. I promise to love you when the sun shines, when the rain falls, in sickness, and health, for richer or poorer until death do us apart."* You pledge your covenant with each other.

One of the words of Scripture, which has all but gone out of style as it pertains to marriage, is the word **Covenant**. There was a time when it was the theme of the Hebrew people. Strong holy men and women of God knew to be in **covenant** with someone, especially with God who has sworn faithfully to fulfill in them every promise He has given, merited the utmost loyalty, commitment, and unyielding dedication.

The wedding vows manufactures deep regard for another, one who has made a solemn oath to stay the course no matter the difficulty. Although our vows rang true at the marriage ceremony at the time we said them, it is evident in today's culture, words, oaths, and promises have little weight and value to them.

In a culture where no one is held accountable for what they say, no longer is their word their bond; the covenant becomes a recluse. Now we say, I didn't mean it, I was just kidding; that's not what I meant; you misinterpreted what I said; I made a mistake or misspoke. Some will flat out deny they said it even with empirical evidence they did; some also use a new term "alternative truth"; what?! Wait! There is no such thing as an alternative truth!

The words in our vows today have no substance, no binding power. They are as light as a kite blowing whichever way the emotional wind does. The words of commitment flutter with the mood of our heart; if the heart doesn't love anymore the words lose their power. In today's society we don't have covenants; we have contracts. A contract is more easily broken than a covenant. A covenant carries a heavier weight of legal consequences and personal affliction in biblical terms.

Covenant vs. Contracts

[22]*"Truth, covenants, and ordinances enable us to overcome fear and face the future with faith." -Russell M. Nelson*

Contracts are broken when one of the parties fails to keep their promise. I once read it described this way- *"If let us say, a patient fails to keep an appointment with a doctor; the doctor is not obligated to call the house and inquire, "Where were you? Why didn't you show up

[22] Russell M. Nelson, *Face the Future with Faith*, The Church of Jesus Christ Latter-Saints, April 2011, February 2020

for your appointment?" He simply goes on to his next patient and has his appointment secretary take note of the patient who failed to keep the appointment. The patient may find it harder the next time to see the doctor because he broke an informal contract. The Bible indicates the covenant is more like the ties of a parent to her child than it is a doctor's appointment. If a child fails to show up for dinner, the parent's obligation, unlike the doctor's, isn't canceled. The parent finds out where the child is and makes sure he's cared for. One member's failure does not destroy the relationship. A covenant puts no conditions on faithfulness. It is the unconditional commitment to love and serve".

"Therefore, shall a man leave his father and mother, and shall cleave unto his wife: and they shall be one flesh." *Again, in the eyes of God, a covenant is binding oneself to another, a gluing together never to break apart.*

In the beginning, marriage was a covenant between a man and a woman which God has joined together. As a *covenan*t marriage is until death do us part. A *contract* converts to, until I don't like you anymore. A contractual understanding of marriage leads to things like no-fault divorce and prenuptial agreements. When you enter marriages with that mindset, in most cases it has ended before it starts. By the way, "No-fault divorce"... someone is at fault!

This institution of marriage God designed with Adam and Eve sets the standard for all weddings to come and because God decreed it He is now a part of it. This now ***holy*** institution is the beginning of all divine ***blessings*** that would flow from God to the family and the world. ***When God brought His Son Jesus into this world, who is the second Adam, He was reestablishing the marriage order; husband to wife, but also Christ to the church–His bride***. Through Christ the Father would set back in order His original intention of marriage. By the way, in Old Testament times it was the father that found the bride for his son; can you see the correlation?.

Let's look at our text (Genesis 2: 21-25). ***"And God caused a deep sleep to fall on Adam, and he slept: and He took one of his ribs, and***

closed up the flesh in its place. Then the rib which the LORD God had taken from man He made into a woman, and He brought her to the man."

Here are the first marriage ceremony and covenant. When God brought Eve to Adam, God was the binding legal authority of that marriage. Anytime a couple is married under the name of God; His name becomes the binding authority over that marriage along with our reciting of vows. It is this observance of His name that we must strive never to taint. Even though Adam and Eve's marriage hit as low as any marriage could reach they nevertheless had a strong covenant with each other and remained married until their death. No marriage in all of humanity has had to endure the strain, burden, worries, and trauma of mankind's "First marriage," and yet, because of God's name and covenant they endured to the end.

*Bruce Shelley, blog *Covenant Not Contract,* February 2nd 2009, I.H. MarshallJesus the Savior, IVP, 1990, p. 275ff

Covenant in God's eyes*:* [34] *Instead, one of the soldiers pierced Jesus' side with a spear, bringing a sudden flow of blood and water." "Not one of his bones will be broken,"*[a] [37] *and, as another scripture says, "They will look on the one they have pierced."* (John 19: 31-37) *NIV*

I believe, in addition to the sacrifice of Jesus on the cross for our sins, He died on the cross for His new Eve, "The Church" ***cut*** from His side. Keep a finger on this word "cut," it will mean something noteworthy later. On the cross, the spear was ***cut*** into the side of Jesus, and blood and water flowed from His side. When God put the first Adam in a deep sleep, it could be perceived as an image of Christ's death. When God ***cut*** Adam open to remove his rib, blood and water were exposed, as it was with Jesus. It was the spear of the soldier that cut the physical body of Jesus, but it was the Spiritual scalpel of the Father that cut out and cut forth the church as Jesus hung on the cross. When God woke Adam up from his sleep, this is a picture illustrating God raised Jesus from the dead. Soon after that, God brings Eve to her husband. Likewise, God *spiritually* took out a bone of Jesus' body and created a new bride, *the* *church*. We could say without stretching too far, those that are in Christ Jesus are the spiritual rib of Jesus. God knew from creation Adam and Eve would spiritually represent the marriage of Christ and the church.

Who and what is the church? ***"all those that My Father gives to Me will come to Me,"*** this is the church. As her Father gave Eve to Adam, He gives us to Jesus (John 6:37). This is the mystery clarified in (Ephesians 5:22-33; 1 Peter 3:1-7).

2 *I saw the Holy City, the new Jerusalem, coming down out of heaven from God, prepared as a* ***bride*** *beautifully dressed for her husband.* (Revelation 21: 2) NIV

Our earthly marriage ought to image the spiritual union of Christ and the Church. We should understand, if we let Jesus dress us and prepare and adorn our marriage, our marriage will be beautiful and able to sustain all hardships, trials, tribulations, afflictions, and calamity. But first and foremost, it is all about the covenant!

Covenant means an alliance of marriage in Malachi 2:14, *("Yet you say, 'For what reason?' Because the LORD has been a witness between you and the wife of your youth, against whom you have dealt treacherously, though she is your companion and your wife by covenant.")*

Elsewhere in (Proverbs 2:17), most commentaries believe this has significant meaning to the betrayal of a covenant of marriage, *"That leaves the companion of her youth, and forgets the covenant of her God."*

[23]Warren Wiersbe writes that the woman described here in (Proverbs 2:17) "*She has no respect for God, because she breaks His law* (Ex. 20:14); she has no respect for her husband because she violates the promises she made to him when she married him. She no longer has a guide or a friend in the Lord or in her husband, because she has taken the path of sin. Anyone who listens to her words and follows her path is heading for the cemetery."

---

[23] Warren Wiersbe, *Bible Exposition Commentary: Old Testament Wisdom and Poetry, Volume 1,*
David C. Cook, 2004, p. 402

When Adam said the words *"This is now bone of my bone, and flesh of my flesh,"* it was his wedding vows. He was acknowledging his commitment to her and his covenant of one-ness.

When Jesus said, *"[28] Come to Me, all you who labor and are heavy laden, and I will give you rest. [29] Take My yoke upon you and learn from Me, for I am gentle and lowly in heart, and you will find rest for your souls. [30] For My yoke is easy, and My burden is light." Matthew 11:28-30.*

Now that's a wedding vow! What a formula for all who trust in Him. To carry the responsibility and the heavy load of life's circumstances for His bride; to be gentle with His bride, to create a space for His bride to feel safe enough to rest in Him. Though both have a yoke- the bride has a yoke to submit, honor, and respect Him. But the husband must make it easy for His bride to submit. The husband has a yoke to love her unconditionally and should be eager to do so. Likewise, the wife must make it easy for the husband to love her. This harness and coupling will fasten them together in the plowing to pull through the tough times of marriage.

Definition of Covenant

*The meaning of the Hebrew word for **covenant** is illustrated in (Genesis 15), the first use of this Hebrew phrase is "**cut covenant**"; often translated "**make [made] a covenant**." The word used here is "*karath*-cut, **beriyth*-covenant." Greek/Hebrew?

"So He (God) said to him (Abram), *"Bring Me a three year old heifer, and a three year old female goat, and a three year old ram, and a turtledove, and a young pigeon." 10 Then he brought all these to Him and cut them in two, and laid each half opposite the other; but he did not cut the birds. 11 And the birds of prey came down upon the carcasses, and Abram drove them away. 12 Now when the sun was going down, a deep sleep fell upon Abram; and behold, terror and great darkness fell upon him. And it came about when the sun had set, that it was very dark, and behold, there appeared a smoking oven and a flaming torch which passed between these pieces. 18*

On that day the LORD ***made*** *(cut = karath) a* ***covenant*** *(beriyth) with Abram, saying, "To your descendants I have given this land, From the river of Egypt as far as the great river, the river Euphrates"* (Ge 15:9-12, 17, 18)

This strange passage illustrates the meaning of a covenant made by passing between the halves of cut flesh. In this case, using bizarre language, Moses illustrates that it was Jehovah alone who moved between the halves of flesh, indicating God cut an *unconditional* covenant with Abram. *The spillage of blood was part of the cutting of this covenant.* God invokes an oath or curse on Himself should He abandon or is unable to keep His covenant with Abraham. In other words, God is saying I will do to Myself as I have done with this dove and pigeon if I forsake My covenant with you. God swears by Himself to keep the covenant terms because nothing is a higher authority. It would seem God is serious about His covenant.

This marriage covenant could also be seen as an illustration of a virgin consummating the marriage. As her husband passes through the cut of her womb, as her blood flowed from her virginity, it became a binding covenant with her husband. In the Old Testament Jewish culture, after the virgin laid with her husband, she kept the bedsheet to prove the consummation of the marriage to bind her husband to a covenant of marriage. Although our society is much different today and hardly anyone values the sanctity of not having sex before marriage, even though this is what God intended and pleases Him; we could stand to learn from this practice of chastity, because when we understand the significance and why it's crucial to do so, hopefully, we will tend to observe it better and stay married until death do us apart.

[24]Charles Spurgeon quotes related to **covenant** "As we are under the covenant of grace, we are secured against ***departing*** from the living God by the sure declaration of the covenant."

---

[24] Charles Spurgeon, *The Lord's Free Man*, The Spirit Life Network, November 2011, February 2020

When we genuinely understand covenant it frees us to be secure in who we are and our responsibility within the bond becomes more transparent and more natural. We can now see through God's eyes a new perspective rather than through the eyes of Fallen man. When we visualize being married to our spouse as we are to Christ this should give a sense of urgency to do all we can to have and maintain a healthy marriage. I sincerely believe this to be crucial to marriage, "covenant," never give up, never quit, as much as it depends on you. When you understand covenant you instantly realize and appreciate the love the Father has for you, what He gave up getting you back and keeping you through all of eternity.

Once I studied and came to the awareness of a covenant marriage, it solidified my mind to fight, fight through all the ups and downs of marriage. Seeing covenant for the first time reminds me of a story I read:

"A color-blind boy's world just got a little brighter,"- the title read. 12-year old Jonathan was learning about color blindness in class when his school's principal came in. The principle, who also suffers from colorblindness, gave Jonathan a pair of special glasses that allow the wearer to see color. Jonathan's reaction was incredibly moving. At first, he gives a little jolt of surprise at his surroundings, which makes the class laugh and applaud. Moments later, Jonathan becomes visibly overwhelmed and breaks down in tears, as the principal comforts him with a hug. To some degree, I relate Jonathan's story to mine. I didn't realize how colorful marriage could be until God gave me glasses to see it through covenant. Even if my marriage never reached the place I dreamed it to be, because of the covenant, I would stay the course for I know my reward in heaven would far outweigh my reward here on earth. It is covenant thinking that gives me staying power when I want to leave.

What about divorce?

In the beginning, it was not so:

Ask yourself a question, "Is it more important to satisfy your will or the will of God?" As it pertains to divorce, Jesus says, in the beginning divorce was not the Father's will! The Bible clearly states that God hates divorce. Most of the time the devil will make us think our marriage is worse than it really is and it prompts us to run toward divorce, but your marriage may not be as bad as you make it out to be. Even if you're not very happy in your marriage right now, happiness is not the main element of marriage. The sacrifice, the journey, the growing together through tough times, are the ingredients to a holy marriage which brings happiness. A marriage will not be happy without it first being holy.

Aristotle said, "All men seek happiness; there are no exceptions." That is true, but was Aristotle married? Just kidding! He was actually. *But what if marriage was designed to make you more holy than more happy?* This quote from Gary Thomas, from his book Sacred Marriage, in my mind makes an interesting point. Marriage will not always be happy, but it should always be a holy covenant.

To love this woman is to love God. To hate this woman is to despise God. How can you say you love God but have grown to hate your wife? (1 John 4:20,21). When you have a clear understanding of how much God hates divorce, and you get divorced, it can seem and feel as though you divorced God. Divorce is often a devastating thing. It affects all involved in a negative way, and women and children, especially, often are hurt the most. Whether their lives change for better or for worse, it's extremely common for women to struggle with emotional trauma after divorce. This could include feelings of failure, sadness, and loneliness, and frequently, women can even fight with depression or anxiety. Children often feel abandoned and discarded, and often feel it's their fault. But divorce affects more than our emotions; it affects our soul.

Once a husband and wife enter into holy matrimony they enter into more than raising a family; they enter into a life-changing covenant, a covenant with each other but more importantly, with God. And for the believer, the child of God, breaking a covenant with God can often bring emptiness, shame, and despair to the soul.

Jesus goes further in (Matthew 5: 31,32) *"It was also said, 'Whoever divorces his wife, let him give her a certificate of divorce.' 32 But I say to you that everyone who divorces his wife, except on the grounds of sexual immorality, makes her commit adultery, and whoever marries a divorced woman commits adultery".* These are severe words from Jesus, thank God for His grace.

[25]Spurgeon comments that in these passages, related to divorce, "Moses insisted upon "a writing of divorcement," that angry passions might have time to cool and that the separation, if it must come, might be performed with deliberation and legal formality. The requirement of a writing was to a certain degree a check upon an evil habit, which was so ingrained in the people that to refuse it altogether would have been useless and would only have created another crime. The law of Moses went as far as it could practically be enforced; it was because of the hardness of their hearts that divorce was tolerated; it was never approved."

[26]Barclay, "The voice of God had said, "I hate divorce" (Malachi 2:16). The Rabbis had the loveliest sayings. "We find that God is long-suffering to every sin except the sin—of unchastity." "Unchastity causes the glory of God to depart." "Every Jew must surrender his life rather than commit idolatry, murder or adultery." "The very altar sheds tears when a man divorces the wife of his youth." The tragedy was that practice fell so far short of the ideal. One thing violated the whole marriage relationship."

---

[25] Study Light, Bible Commentaries William Barclay's Daily Study Bible, Matthew 19, Charles Spurgeon, 2001-2020

[26] Study Light, Bible Commentaries William Barclay's Daily Study Bible, Matthew 19, William Barclay, 2001-2020

Chapter Seventeen

ENTERING THE TEMPLE OF LOVE

"Inside the chaos, build a temple of love" -Rune Lazuli

"A marriage may be made in heaven, but the maintenance must be done on earth."–Anonymous

19 Or do you not know that your body is the temple of the Holy Spirit
who is in you, whom you have from God, and you are not your own?
20 For you were bought at a price; therefore glorify God in your body [a]
and in your spirit, which are God's. (I Corinthians 6:19-21)

After God created Adam, He placed him in a perfect environment and had a perfect spiritual relationship with God; Adam had all the possessions he wanted; it was indeed Eden. And yet, God said, "It is not good for man to be alone." He was still void of intimacy. This has always puzzled me. Why would Adam need intimacy when he was spiritually intimate with God? Isn't that our whole quest, to have such a relationship with God that we are one with Him? Adam did possess spiritual intimacy with God but he was also flesh in nature. And in his physical environment he was void of intimacy, incomplete and incompatible with any other creature.

Through Eve, God was essentially giving Himself to Adam in another form, a beautiful form that would be physically compatible with him. When husband and wife come together as one in the joy and pleasure of sex, they reach a place of fulfilling phyical and spiritual intimacy. This is a beautiful picture of how much God loves mankind and how we are to love Him. *Love the Lord God with all of your heart, mind, and soul.* God is a jealous God, and He wants all of us. In turn, Adam is to love Eve as he loves God, not above or ahead of God, but with absolute devotion to please her as he wills to please God. Other than Jesus on the cross, which died for His bride, there is no greater picture of love than marriage, no greater joy than marriage.

The husband and wife can experience the full pleasure and satisfaction of intimacy because they literally become one flesh, spiritually, emotionally, physiologically, and physically as the Husband and the Bride become one. This action of both spiritual and physical intercourse is designed by God to be pleasurable, to enjoy one another until death does them part. When the husband or wife is deprived of this union of sex, in a sense, they deprive one another of what brings joy to God, the spiritual and physical union of the one-fleshness between man and woman. It also makes one destitute, usually, more so the husband, and opens up a door for Satan to come in and cause pornography and adultery. In fact, 1 Corinthians 7:5 commands us not to deprive each other of this kind of intimacy. If a husband and wife are not intimate, how can they be fully intimate with God? I'm not speaking of a physical condition that prohibits intimacy, but the unwillingness to adhere to what is surely a biblical command.

[27]Sheila Wray Gregoire, writes in her article "The most common conflict when it comes to sex in marriage is about frequency: one spouse tends to want more sex than the other, and this leads to the higher-libido spouse feeling unloved. Why doesn't my wife want to show me love? Why doesn't my husband desire me? Then this starts a vicious circle where the other spouse thinks, "is that all they want from me? Am I just an object?" And it goes downhill from there."- **What Does 1 Corinthians 7:5–Do Not Deprive Each Other–Really Mean?**

---

[27] Sheila Wray Gregoire, *Libido, Marriage, Resolving Conflict, Sex, Sexual Intimacy,* To Love Honor And Vaccum, October 2012, February 2020

How does this relate to being intimate with God? Jesus says go into your prayer closet, close the door, and what you ask in the dark, "the secret place, the private place," it will be given to you in the light. When we pray, we enter into God's most precious holy and private place. There's an intimacy that takes place between Creator and His creation; we enter into God's HOLY of holies and begin to release prayer, praise, and worship and the fruit of our prayer is an intimate time with God which is designed to produce a new life, a new way of living. After Jesus died on the cross after He gave all He had- His life, the curtain in the temple was torn from top to bottom so we could have access to God's most precious private and holy place. In Old Testament times, Only the High priest entered the Holy of holies; not anyone could enter, they had to be chosen by God to be part of this private encounter and confidential embrace. Prayer is so essential, it's mandatory in the life of a believer.

The Bible tells us that we ought always to pray, pray without ceasing. In prayer is the quietness God wants with you, to receive you, accept you, and love you. In prayer, God opens Himself to you and you to Him. If we don't pray on a continuous basis we deprive God of this intimate time with us.

When a woman is ready to receive a man into her most private place, it becomes prepared to receive the encounter. If the woman is not prepared and the man tries to enter her forcefully, it is not a pleasant experience for the woman. When we try to force our way into God's Holy of holies without giving our life to Christ, which is the instrument by which we enter, it is not an enjoyable experience to God, the Father's holy place is not prepared to receive you. Without consent that act of force is considered rape. It is a strange fire to God.

Nothing is more naked, exposed, revealing, and private than when a woman gives herself to the one she loves. When a man has entered this most holy sanctum he is entering on holy ground. Her most human frailty is known; nothing is kept back. This is the problem with premarital sex; the man has trodden on holy ground with boots. Her virginity is a treasured sacred place and is to be discovered only by the one who is willing to sacrifice all he has for this pearl of love. But when her solemn place of love becomes uncovered before its time, he uncovers secrets he had no right to discover. You've entered a holy place that was not meant for you. Without vows, without commitment, without humility to be granted in, such an entrance is sacrilege. When premarital sex is engaged it is not protected by holiness and it will soon breed contempt. There is no incentive to love without holiness because there is not a necessity to love. Once you are married, there is a necessity to love, a command to love, and it will require taking up a cross, a sacrifice every day. Marriage destroys us! It should destroy us, destroy our ego and selfishness.

His body belongs to her and hers to his (1 Cor. 7:1-9): Usually for most God-fearing women, when they fall in love with a man and marry him, they want to surrender all to him while feeling safe in doing so. All that she guards as valuable and delicate, she is willing to surrender it, that's true love. What happiness and joy that is to the soul, to surrender to the one you love knowing they would not hurt, damage, misuse, or abuse it in any way. When a woman can surrender her body, not as a pleasure piece, but has a *holy* vessel to the man she loves, a man that knows her, cares for her, and loves her as Christ loves her, is there anything that could make a woman happier? When she comes to a place so comfortable and trusting in her husband that she no longer owns her body but gives it up to her husband entirely to do as he wills; wow! What freedom, what joy, what happiness. When she can surrender in this fashion to her husband it is because she has first surrendered her will and her body to God.

"*The Bible presents a woman as a strong image bearer of God, able to stand against the world, powerfully influencing men and culture... as she lives the life God created her to live.*"- [28]Gary Thomas

---

[28] Gary Thomas, *Sacred Marriage*, Zondervan Publisher, August 2015

Chapter Eighteen FINANCIAL ILLITERACY

"We buy things we don't need with money we don't have in order to impress people we don't like." -Dave Ramsey

"Why do you spend money for what is not bread, and your wages for what does not satisfy?" (Isaiah 55:2)

Financial illiteracy, poor stewardship, complacency to budget, and meager money management can often lead to an unhappy marriage and ministry and an unbalanced life. If the average wife does not feel secure financially she will harbor a lack of trust toward her husband. Not that she needs to see millions in the bank account, but she must be a part of the long-term goal for the comfort and viability of the family. Financial security will allow her to not stress over finances, giving her more time and energy to be her husband's helpmeet. Likewise, pastors must be a good steward with God's money or the church and home will suffer in some form or another. Although I am learning to be a better money manager at home, when it comes to the Church's money, I find it prudent to surround myself with people who are better at it than I am.

Like most people, I've always wanted to be successful financially, however, I was never taught the principles or took it upon myself to learn fiscal responsibility. It's no excuse, but I'm a cloth cut from my father when it comes to money. My father was brilliant in some areas but fell way short in financial responsibility. He was rather light-footed about money, whimsical if you will. He had a well-paying Job but lived payday to payday. As I recall, he never had a bank account or savings account and never invested and kept what money he had hidden in the house. There were some things he would spare no expense for; food, cigarettes, clothes, guns, and Gordon's Gin. My father worked for the railroad as a chef and, at times, a waiter for the passenger train Amtrak. He loved to cook, and I loved to eat our favorite meal, New York strip steak, asparagus, mash potatoes, and Texas toast; that brings back memories, man! I'm getting hungry. If he had a full refrigerator, an entire bottle of Gin, packs of cigarettes, his 357-magnum gun under his pillow and a little cash to spend in his pocket, he was content. He was a simple man, never owning a car, ever, he didn't know how to drive.

My older brother, who I lived with during the school months in Abilene, Texas, made a good living as a Life Insurance Salesman. He always had money, but everybody labeled him stingy, because well, he was! Not that he loved money, he was just parcial who he lent it to. So, I didn't have great examples and this bad habit of financial irresponsibility follows me to this day. Although I have become much better, the tenacity and discipline to save all I can still isn't my best skill and it has caused major distrust and division in our marriage. My very frugal wife is the opposite; she handles money well and has better examples in her family. Her father is a retired Colonel and has invested well and passed his financial wisdom and knowledge to his children.

She can't comprehend my seeming lack of concern for the family's financial security, and that causes her not to feel not-so-safe in this area; therefore, I have placed her in a position of trying to do it on her own. I wish I could go back in time and start over in this area. I'm burdened by my failure in this, and putting that weight on her shoulders isn't fair. I recognize my fault but I'm not a dead-beat husband or dad. For 30 years, we've been married; I've made a middle to upper-income salary, and until I quit my job and became fulltime in ministry, I was making six figures. We've never been without a home, without a car, without food, clothes, etc. By most of America's standards we've lived a comfortable life.

Of course, there have been times, the electricity has been cut off, or a car payment was missed, or we didn't pay our taxes on time. Not because God has not blessed me with the means but because I wasn't a good steward. She has had ample reason not to trust me. Over the last five years I've become much more focused and intent on building a financial future for my family, and I pray she sees my efforts.

Money management can be tied to one's character and stomach; *if a man does not work, he does not eat:* even Adam had a job. Work has never been an issue for me. One thing my dad did teach me is how to work, to be accountable, dependable and to excel in everything I do. I am competitive by nature, extremely competitive. That attribute has boded me well most of the time; however, it also brings out the worst in me at times.

I received a partial track scholarship to attend Wayland Baptist University. High-Jump was my specialty; I stood 5'10 ½" but could High-Jump 6' 10". That's right! While there, I tried out for the Basketball team and made it as a walk-on. The Basketball program paid for the other half of my school with its partial scholarship, however I dropped out after a year.

Despite being a poor student all my life, poor as in not academically inclined, I had reached a goal I never thought I would or could. My Dad didn't have the money to send me to college and because of low academic scores I was kicked off the Track and Basketball team, which meant I lost the scholarships and had to leave college.

I graduated from High School, but barely. I didn't like school, I never have, and it was difficult for me. I didn't have dyslexia, ADHD, or any learning disorder but was never taught learning skills. My parents never read to me or with me. My mom passed when I was five years old, and my dad was always on the road. I lived with my brother and his family and it was more of the same. My sister-in-law is incredibly smart and taught her children well, but it must have been challenging for her to teach me since I was way behind for my age. She did her best, but by the time I started first grade I was at least two grades behind the other children. I hadn't learned the basics of reading or anything else, and I was so scared and intimidated that the first day at school I ran away. From that point, school was a struggle and a blur and not an enjoyable experience.

I don't remember any of my teachers except two; my seventh grade English teacher Mrs. Gilbreth, which I had a crush on, and my High school Basketball coach, who I did not have a crush on, Coach Dub Peirce. He was a good coach and seemed to care for my wellbeing. Mrs. Gilbreth was extremely nice to me. On the first day of school she asked all the kids what she should call us, by our first or middle name? I chose my middle, Louis. I think I chose Louis because it allowed me to start fresh and be who I wanted to be not who I thought I was, dumb! From that day on, she called me Louis, and I liked it.

To some extent, she helped me with my reading; I was a pitiful reader and afraid to read aloud. I'm sure it was because of an unfortunate event when my sister-in-law was trying to teach me to read. One evening she instructed me to go to my room and read a children's book and not to come out until I finished. I just couldn't do it, some words I could understand but others frustrated and intimidated me. Time and time again I was sent to my room. Finally, she was so frustrated she sent me to the room to sit in the dark as a punishment for not learning to read. I don't blame her at all and till this day I have never mentioned the darkroom, I don't need to either. We all make mistakes, and her life was pretty grueling at that time. I'm sure she doesn't remember the matter and that's okay with me. I love her dearly today, and she is my favorite sister-in-law and a dedicated Christian woman, wife, and mother.

Having a fear of reading until my senior year in High school, I was terrified to read in front of people. However, that year I took a drama class for an elective course. I don't know why I chose this class, it was probably the only one available. I didn't know what it was about, I didn't care, I just wanted to complete it and graduate. After a few days in the class the teacher explained we would stand in groups and perform a mini skit of whatever we choose. Wait, WHAT! No way this is happening, you want me to do WHAT? I exclaimed in my scared inner voice to myself. Our group chose the story, The Big Bad Wolf and the Three Pigs, and wanted me to play the Big Bad Wolf. Fortunately, there was very little reading, mostly dramatization. When it was our turn we stood in front of the whole class and I was so nervous my knees were shaking, I could barely stand it. As the others finished reciting their lines it was time for me to deliver my part and to my surprise, I NAILED IT!–that's right! They loved me. Little Denzel was born. They told me a star was born, and after that day everyone wanted me on their team. We all have hidden potential not yet discovered; all of us are born with purpose and destiny and sometimes facing our fears and challenges brings out those gifts. God gives us glimpses of open-door opportunities throughout our lives but it's up to us to walk through them.

From that point on I was never afraid, anxious sometimes, but never afraid to stand up in front of a crowd, whether to read or what have you, I was delivered. Little did I know, God was preparing me to speak in front of hundreds and even thousands of people. So, here I am, a Pastor, speaking and reading in front of people every Sunday.

I never wanted to be a preacher or a Pastor; my older brother was and I saw the burden and liability it had on his family. I think anyone who says they want to be a Pastor doesn't have a great understanding of the calling. They see the respect and honor, fame and fortune of some preachers, the accolades during pastor appreciation and think the work is easy. It is not! This is a job you must be called by God to do. The natural man has no place in the pulpit. The fame and fortune seeker have no place shepherding God's people. The well-intentioned humanist has no place in the spiritual house of God. Shepherding God's sheep is not a vocation; it is a calling. It is an appointment before the foundation of the world; it is your destiny and your purpose. Those called, have been on the road to be a Pastor from the day you were born. Pastors are not made, they are born. You might not have known it or even wanted it, but God all along the way put certain people and experiences in your path to prepare you for the most critical job in the world. To work for and with God to save souls.

God is not leaving the saving of souls to chance. He is not hoping someone will take the position. He has assured those He has called will yield to the job. And though He has called fallible people, His grace has secured them to complete a good work in them. He has equipped them, endowed them with incredible spiritual gifts and power to finish the job; "those whom He has called will come to Jesus." Those that are called will sell their field to find the one great pearl; they will count the cost and are willing to leave all behind. Someone once said, "Some were called, some were sent, but some, just got up and went." Don't be a "went" preacher but a called one.

Bottom line, whatever career you pursue, learn to be financially responsible. The issue with most people is they think they don't have the skill or they grew up on the wrong side of the tracks or their environment prohibits them from financial freedom. A wise man told me once, *"People don't have a lack of resources, they have a lack of resourcefulness."*

Chapter Nineteen

Three Mysterious Female Messengers from God

"Do not forget to show hospitality to strangers, for by so doing some people have shown hospitality to angels without knowing it."
(Hebrew 13:2) NIV

"There must be more to life than this"

At the ranch, I'm thinking, "It is strange. I never wanted to preach, let alone pastor a church." But now, for 13 years, God has helped me and encouraged me to continue shepherding His people. I had a peculiar path to this calling gift of Pastor/Teacher. It started when I was 34 years old. I had climbed the Retail Corporate ladder to a position of Area Supervisor for a shoe store chain, at the time, the only African American to do so at this company, so I was told. However, after about 15 years in the shoe business life started to change. I had lost my enthusiasm and drive. I began to have issues with upper management even though I was still performing at a high level; something just wasn't right in my soul. It felt empty, I had lost my focus and ambition. Soon, I was getting passed over for higher positions and the CEO who used to call and chat from time to time stopped calling. Opportunities begin to close; finally, business took a downturn. Frustrated, I begin to ask myself, *there must be more to life than this?* Have you ever been there?

I began trying to educate myself thinking that would solve the problem. Never being an avid reader, I knew I needed to improve my reading and writing skills so my quest for self-improvement began. I started reading motivational books, self-help books, books on grammar and writing, but nothing was filling the void. Uneducated and with only one disappointing year of College, I've always had a complex about my schooling. Around academic and well-educated people I either tried to avoid long conversations fearing my lack of vocabulary and knowledge would soon be apparent, or I would pretend to understand subject matters beyond my intellect, which made me feel awkward and clumsy. I was very thankful to have achieved this level of success in my job and considered myself blessed despite my education. After 15 years on the job, a turning point stared me right in the face. I grappled for a long time about quitting, afraid to do so thinking I wouldn't find another job that paid as much because of my lack of social media or computer skills. The world was different than when I entered the workplace 15 years earlier. Man, the devil really knows how to deflate your confidence.

I eventually built enough confidence to quit my job hoping and praying I'd find something that would fill this void in my soul. Soon I was hired at a jewelry store, a different product, same game. Sales are sales no matter the product and I was good at it. This job came with a higher salary and within a year I climbed the ladder to store manager. With my confidence back and things looking better, you would think I would be happy, but I wasn't. The new job filled my natural desires but my soul was thirsty for more. Oh, there were times I enjoyed life, God blessed my family and me. But there was still space unfulfilled, a purpose I didn't know about; my life felt empty, unfinished, and I couldn't fill it no matter what I did.

I should have been content with a new job, beautiful wife and family and all are healthy, but the tug, "*there's more to life than this*" would not leave my spirit. Jesus said, *"I came that you might have life and have it more abundantly."* (John 10:10). **I was living, but I didn't have life!**

Here comes the mysterious, odd part. While working for the jewelry store I joined the Amway business hoping to fill this void with natural means, more mammon and material stuff. The company suggested we go to conferences that were geared to raise your excitement and enthusiasm, pump you up and motivate you to build a wealthy business. My kind of ticket! I was ready and super pumped about the potential; there was legitimate money to be made but I just didn't have the patience or money to build it. We tried it for almost three years, but it never panned out for us. I met a few who succeeded; It was fun, met lots of good people, but Faith and I finally moved on. I'd talked her into joining the business with me and reluctantly, she did. When it didn't work out it was another reason for her not to trust me. I really believed we could do it; I'm optimistic that way, but it just didn't work out.

But something amazing, life-changing, happened to me while attending one of the conferences of about 2,000 people. One of the speakers was giving a heartfelt speech about how he came to know Christ and that Jesus had made him a better man. He was not a preacher, but as he spoke I felt the atmosphere change, it was a moving speech. It affected many men in that auditorium that day, but for me, it was life changing. I felt my heart warmth, my emotions melted into a sense of helplessness, and I cried out to Jesus that day to take my life into His hands, and He did. That day, at an Amway conference, I gave my life to Christ. I was chasing money and ran into the Lord. Jesus can call you anywhere, anytime, any-place, using anybody. "AMWAY"–really? Yes sir, the honest to God's truth. Thank you, Amway!

A few weeks later, my hunger and thirst for God grew exponentially; I began to saturate my mind and spirit with study after study of God's word. It consumed me; I couldn't get enough. I finally joined a church in Houston where I knew the pastor, Remus, and Mia Wright of A Fountain of Praise Church. Now there's an incredible story of a man and his wife, Mia, the author of "Unthinkable." God used them to grow their church from about 150 people to somewhere in the neighborhood of 15,000. Pastor Remus baptized me and my Christian journey began.

Faith and I, along with our little daughter Brooke lived in the Houston area for about four years. However, we both wanted to move back into our house in Round Rock, Texas, which we leased out while we were away. When we finally moved back to Round Rock I was transferred with the jewelry company, but took a demotion because only a sales position was open. Soon after moving back to Round Rock I began to search for a church; I would travel each Sunday near and far and found nothing that met our needs. One day while at work, a little old lady, "Mrs. Parker" walks into the jewelry store, and right off the bat I knew she was a Christian; she had a light within her that shined.

I said boldly, "Hi, can I ask you a question?" She replied, "Yes." I asked, "Where do you attend church?" She told me, and it turns out the church wasn't far from my house. I visited a couple of Sundays in a row and was moved by the pastor's message. One Sunday, he spoke about "Reluctant Boat People," using the text where Peter said, "Bid me to come, Lord," it was a good sermon. I've borrowed it a few times myself.

The next Sunday, I joined the church but I never really discussed it with my wife or as a family. Once again my stupidity and lack of consideration for my wife's thoughts and emotions seem to be a theme with me. It's not that I am maliciously trying to hurt my wife, I'm not that kind of person, but something in me, a flaw, seems to think it's okay not to include my wife in major decisions like that.

The pastor and I hit it off quickly and we became really good friends. We played golf together and he was just as competitive as I was. We would brag all the time about who shot better scores and truth be told, I did! He would disagree. After a couple of months, he asked me to help in the youth ministry. That is certainly not my calling, but I did it, and it was proper training for me. Within the year the Lord sent two younger men who were best friends; they joined the church and loved kids and youth ministry; it was their calling. Quickly and eagerly I relinquished charge over that ministry. After that the pastor assigned me over the men's ministry and I really enjoyed that assignment. I have a heart for men who are lost but trying to do better. I was at that post for about six months but God was tugging on my heart for more of me.

Be careful, you may be entertaining angels:

What I'm about to tell you might seem strange, but remember, there are times when heaven and earth collide when heaven invades the natural laws of man and there are no adequate words to describe it.

We had an event at our church one evening and the pastor asked me to preside over the service. After it was over, and this is where it gets interesting, a *"little old lady"* that I had never seen before and never have seen again since, approached me. Though many people were still socializing the atmosphere was if no one else was in the church, even though I could see them. It's as though I was temporarily in a trance but I didn't realize it at the time. She said to me, "Son, the Lord told me to tell you, He wants you to preach." Honestly, those were her only words. After that, I can't remember her walking away and I don't remember her staying. You should be careful what people say God told them to tell you; most of the time, it's not God. I'll just leave it at that. But it was something peculiar, strange and unusual about the *"little old lady."* However, I didn't take what she said very seriously. She had the wrong person, I wasn't about to preach, no way Jose! My brother Jerry who is a pastor and has the spirit of discernment like no one I have known, several years earlier while I was giving an Amway presentation in his office, told me I would be a preacher one day. I thought he was crazy and applied the same thought to the little old lady and didn't think much more about it.

Several months later my pastor asked me to consider being a Deacon; I was honored. A few months after my training I was ordained. After my ordination ceremony, another, but different.... Wait for it... *"little old lady,"* that I had never seen before and till this day never seen again, came down the aisle of the church and said to me, "Son the Lord told me to tell you, He wants you to preach"; those were the only words she spoke.

Okay, this is getting a little eerie. She seemed to, I don't want to use the word "disappear" from my presence, but I don't remember her leaving or staying, it is a blur just like the first little old lady; I can't explain it, there are no words to describe it.

Now I'm a little freaked out but I tell no one, not even my wife. Moreover, the little old lady's words are vibrating in my soul and I can't dismiss them away as I did the first time. The weight of the words are more substantial this time; I begin to contemplate the matter seriously.

Sunday after Sunday, while our pastor is preaching the Holy Spirit would speak to my heart and say, "This is what I want you to do." Indicating, God wanted me to preach. I wrestled with it for another nine months not wanting to hear God's voice. I try and rationalize what has happened and what is occurring within my spirit.

One Sunday my family and I travel to my hometown Abilene TX, to visit my brother's church and his family. A lady was preaching, not as old as the other two mysterious "*little old ladies*" that approached me earlier with a message to preach. This woman was probably in her fifties; she preached a sermon, "Throw Your Trash Away." At the end of her sermon she had a large trash can in the middle of the church and asked for anyone who wanted to, to come and imagine throwing their trash, "sin" in the garbage. A line begins to form and God is tugging on my heart to get up, I resisted as long as I could; finally, I'm not sure why I stand up and get in line. I'm third to the last person in line and all those in front of me are throwing their imaginary sin in the garbage. As they walk by the trash can she kept preaching as they set back down; as I approach, I go through the motion of throwing my sin away in the trash can, she catches my arm, about ten people had gone before me but she touched none of them. She grabbed my arm, looked me in the face... wait for it.... "Young man, the Lord wants me to tell you that you are going to preach and pastor His church." Are you as dumbfounded as I was when she said that to me? Her proclamation was a little different; it went from God wants you to preach, to you are going to preach and pastor His church.

Later that evening we drove back home; you can imagine I was a little rattled. The next day I spoke to my pastor about the incident; he recommended I go home and pray and get back with him when I've confirmed it with God. "Auh, I thank He has confirmed it," I thought, but I wasn't sure. Nothing like this has ever happened to me in my life. This was so over the top, so, well, spiritual; I simply didn't know better.

I went home and prayed a prayer I once heard my brother say he prayed when the Lord called him as a young teen. He said the electricity was disconnected in the house he lived in with our grandfather because they didn't have enough money to pay the bill. It was cut off for a few weeks. My brother prayed to the Lord in the dark and asked God, if He was truly calling him to preach and to give him a sign. He prayed for the lights to be turned on, and when he opened his eyes, they were. He began his calling to ministry that day and has served the Lord for sixty years.

So, I began to pray the same prayer in my den with the lights turned off. When I opened my eyes the room was still dark, the lights were not on. I am devastated. I really believed God was calling me; I'd just told my pastor God was calling me to preach. How would that make me look if He wasn't? I'm distraught and honestly, mad at God that He didn't answer my prayer. I head off to bed and I'm so worked up it's hard for me to sleep, I finally do. I'm not sure what time I went to bed or fell asleep but before I went to bed the bedroom light was off, Faith is already in the bed sleeping.

Sometime that night, not sure what time, I am awakened, as I look at the foot of my bed I see a man clothed in a tremendously almost blinding white robe. He's huge, about eight feet tall it seems, his hair was white or gold but I couldn't make out his face. I can see the face, and yet I can't. What is puzzling to me is, you would think I would be afraid but I'm not. I was in a sense of awe-ness, and the room felt as if it were in another dimension. He never says a word, but suddenly, as I lie there, I began to lift off my bed about three feet. I'm not frightened but extremely curious about what's going on. Then, a feeling, a cleansing if you will begin to rush through me. It's hard to explain with words; it's an experience words can't describe, but I'll do my best-

Once I had to go to the emergency room for severe stomach pain. I had never felt pain that bad before; it was excruciating. The doctors tried a couple of different kinds of medicines, but nothing worked. Finally, they had to give me, I believe it was Vicodin intravenously.

Now, I had never been drunk, taken any kind of narcotic, smoke weed, or any drugs for that matter, I had never been high and never wanted to be. But this stuff was amazing; as the Vicodin entered my bloodstream there was a warmth and euphoria that gently moved effortlessly from the top of my head to my feet and all the pain instantly went away. That is about as close to describing what happened that night in my bedroom; it's as though all my sins were washed away. I believe I experienced the presence of the Angel of the Lord in my bedroom. It was as if he *allowed* me to *feel* all the [forgiveness] of sin being cleansed from my body. I could feel the cleansing start from my head all the way to my feet. I felt the Lord consecrating me, and as He did, a smile came upon my face; it was exhilarating and heavenly, all that I searched for, all the emptiness was now gone. It's as though the words that were spoken to (Ezekiel 36:25-27) happened to me:

25 *"Then will I sprinkle clean water upon you, and ye shall be clean: from all your filthiness, and from all your idols, will I cleanse you.* 26 *A new heart also will I give you, and a new spirit will I put within you: and I will take away the stony heart out of your flesh, and I will give you an heart of flesh.* 27 *And I will put my spirit within you, and cause you to walk in my statutes, and ye shall keep my judgments, and do them."*

I looked at my wife to see if she was witnessing this. Nope! She's fast asleep. The angel begins to let me down to the bed gently, then he is gone. I woke up and wondered was it a dream? Was it an illusion? In my heart I know it wasn't, but it wasn't in this dimension either. I can identify with Paul, *"Whether in the body I do not know, or whether out of the body I do not know, God knows."* Now by no means am I equating my experience with Paul's and I went up to the third heaven as Paul did.

I'm merely saying, God, permitted me to experience something extraordinary, SPIRITUAL, remarkable and would anchor me throughout my ministry during turbulent times. Oh, I almost forgot; get this, when I opened my eyes, the lights were on in my bedroom. I don't know who turned them on; it wasn't me. God did answer my prayer; the way He wanted to.

I will never forget those experiences. I believe the first two "little old ladies" were angels, and the last lady was an earthly confirmation of my call. While angels generally appear as men in Scripture, Zechariah 5:9 may suggest this is not always the case. The two mystical women messengers mentioned in this passage are not specifically called angels, but they are clearly agents of God. Interestingly, God used women in my calling; was it because I lost my mother at such a young age? Perhaps He was preparing me not to have preconceived and preconceptions about women preachers? Just a thought! Perhaps both.

A Phone Call from God!

A Few years after those experiences another supernatural move of God happened. It was weighing heavily on my heart to pastor God's church; I didn't want to, but the pull and tug to do so were evident. I told my pastor what was being impressed on my heart, his directions again were to pray.

Later, in the middle of that week I began to pray early that morning as I had done the last three days with no answer from the Lord. I prayed, "Lord, if you really want me to pastor Your church, then send someone to tell me, if I pastor a church, they will follow me." Now, what are the odds, that out of the blue, somebody would do that exact thing? Well, at about three o'clock that same day I get a phone call from one of the brothers where I attend church.

We had fellowshipped a few times during the Men's bible study, but that was about the extent of our relationship. He says, "Reverend, I don't know why I'm calling you today, but three weeks ago, God told me to tell you if you start a church, I will follow you." ARE YOU KIDDING ME!

I had just asked God at 6am that morning for this sign, at 3pm this Christian brother called me and said God told him three weeks before, to tell me the very thing I prayed for before I even prayed for it. "COME ON MAN... you're making this stuff up." I'm telling you, it happened just the way I described it. On top of that, no one knew I was praying on this matter except my pastor and me.

Chapter Twenty
PRAYER CHANGES THINGS

"Therefore I tell you, whatever you ask for in prayer, believe that you have received it, and it will be yours." (Mark 11:24)

"Pray on it, pray over it, but most of all, pray through it."- Unknown

A man went on a nature walk. A bear began to chase him, so he climbed a tree. As he was climbing he slipped down into the bear's arms. He prayed, "Lord let this be a Christian bear." The bear said, "Lord, thank you for this food."

At the ranch, I spend much time in prayer. This chapter is about the most potent force in the universe in bringing about balance. I cannot underestimate its importance for the child of God, especially one called into ministry. To get an understanding of the power God has put within us and in our hands, we must believe and discipline ourselves to PRAYER.

All that I am now, the motivation to go to the ranch to spend more time with God, to search for answers to my troubled marriage and ministry, all of my efforts to hear from God and draw closer to the Lord Jesus Christ, and writing this book, began with prayer. In addition, I have found, *"Your greatest battles are won on your knees."*

I was always told to pray from my youth but never taught to pray, other than the Lord's Prayer. Called into ministry by the Lord, the intention to pray was placed upon my heart, so instinctively, I knew to pray but praying with power and authority, I was not having great success. I thought the mere act of prayer or repetition prayer would warrant results. I had no idea that prayer was hard work! By the grace of God, He heard my feeble prayers and had compassion on my lack of knowledge on the matter of prayer and granted me some success in prayer, but I knew in my soul that there was more; more power, more authority, more progress to be had. However, I didn't know how to attain it. This trip to the ranch allowed me to acquire a correct understanding of the power of prayer. Astonishing moves of God happened those three days at the ranch, which set me on the path to take prayer seriously, to work at it, and believe in it.

[29]E.M. Bounds, in my mind, this generation's foremost authority on prayer, says, *"In any study of the principle and procedure of prayer, of its activities and enterprises, first place, must, of necessity, be given to faith. It is the initial quality in the heart of any man who essays to talk to the unseen, he must, out of sheer helplessness, stretch forth hands of faith. He must believe, he must believe where he cannot prove. In the ultimate issue, prayer is simply faith, ' '"Moreover: when faith ceases to pray, it ceases to live."*

I have found that nothing is impossible in faithful prayer because nothing is impossible with God. Prayer must be saturated with faith, for it is impossible to please God without it. And if God is not pleased with it, He will not be moved to move mountains in it. When we banish from the soul, doubt and project our faith on God then all that is asked in prayer according to the will of Father will be answered.

I'm reminded of what Jesus says, *"Therefore I say unto you, What things so-ever ye desire when ye pray, believe that ye receive them, and ye shall have them."* (Mark 11:24). I had read this verse many times but it

---

[29] E.M. Bounds, *The Complete Works of E.M. Bounds on Prayer*, Baker Books, 2000, p. 13

never impacted me as it did when I began to study prayer. I've had faith, I've walked by faith, I knew of faith, but to tie faith and prayer together as *inseparable* was not as clear; there was a vagueness, a haziness how it worked. There was always a "what if to my prayer?".

I knew God was willing and able to answer my prayer, but, what if because of my sin, would He not? What if because of my unworthiness, would He not, or what if it's not the right time, would He not? So many "what if's" proceeded my requests. It finally dawned on me that the "what if's was a form of unbelief. Nowhere in the Bible does it leave room for "what if's in our prayer request. When I understood this revelation my prayer was freed from doubt, it blossomed into a stronger faith that strengthens my prayers, I was no longer handicapped about will God do it? I knew within me, He would. "*Believe* that ye shall receive them, and ye shall have them." (Mark 11:24). Wow! what a concept. So simple, and yet it blows my mind.

Faith in what you pray is the principal character in the heart of the believer, and yet, it is prayer that keeps our faith concrete. Prayer is what prepares the soul to go from faith to faith, the human spirit to move from challenges to challenges knowing inevitably the victory is yours in due time.

What if you were blind, whether by birth or malady and for the first time you hear about a man that can heal you by simply touching or even speaking to you? Oh, the other caveat is, your healing would be according to *your* faith. The Bible hasn't been written yet, the church hasn't been established yet, no medical instruments or medicine of the twenty first century have been invented yet; what kind of faith would you have? This is precisely the case in (Mat. 9:28). Jesus says, *"Believe ye that I am able to do this?"* they said unto Him, "Yea, Lord." Then touched He their eyes, saying, *"According to your faith be it unto you."* And their eyes were opened.

Amazing! What faith these simple men had. Their condition and situation humbled them to cry out to Jesus, they set aside pride, smugness or self-importance, embarrassment, bitterness, self-pity, and lay it all down at the feet of Jesus and said, without hesitation, "Yes Lord."

How pleased God must have been to grant their request and how enthusiastic Jesus must have been to produce this miracle. Could it be that simple? Is it that simple? Surely something more is required, surely our own merit must be weighed. In fact, it is that simple. Only belief! Faith is required, and faith is not of yourself; it is the gift of God (Ephesians 2:8). God not only demands faith in His encounter with mankind's requests but He has also given it as a gift for which He requires. He gives us faith freely! Therefore, we are to open and activate the gift of faith combined with prayer and have no "what if's" attached to it.

A righteous man's prayers will be answered, he must not only have faith he must not only pray, but he must also be an honest man, for the righteous man's prayers avails much. A man that loves the Lord commandments and abides in them is well-pleasing to the Lord. The Lord-God is not in the habit of answering prayers to the unredeemed and the wicked, the depraved and immoral man but with those, He is pleased. To do God's will is essential to true faith; obedience is paramount when calling on God in prayer. We must be doers of the Word, not hearers only. "Speak, Lord, I will go; send me," should be every Christians prayer.

Faith prepares the heart for the unavoidable delays in some prayer. *But though it tarries He will come*. We love to say, "He might not come when you want Him, but He is always on time," but do you live by that principle?

[30]*One day John Wesley was walking with a troubled man who expressed his doubt as to the goodness of God. He said, "I do not know what I shall do with all this worry and trouble." At the same moment Wesley saw a cow looking over a stone wall. "Do you know," asked Wesley, "why that cow is looking over the wall?" "No," said the man who was worried. Wesley said,*

---

[30] Gregg Rustulka, *On John Wesley*, Sermon Central, March 29, 2008, February 2020

"The cow is looking over the wall because she cannot see through it. That is what you must do with your wall of trouble—look over it and avoid it."

I am convinced, "Faith" enables us to look past our circumstances and focus on Christ, to look over the valley of doubt to the hills which comes our help.

My wife and I have been married at this point for 30 years. This book is being written because of our ups and downs of marriage and the struggles of becoming "One flesh" as God has commanded. There are many reasons this has not occurred yet and I write throughout the book the reasons why; but I would have you to know, because of prayer, because of faith in prayer, God has kept us together. Often I wanted to quit, move out, separate from my wife but prayer has saved me. Prayer has held me up, encouraged me to stay the course to anticipate a change in our situation. And if the change does not come today, the next day is another opportunity for God to show up and change me, my wife, and our marriage. He is never too late; He is always on time. If it had not been for prayer I would have left my wife and family. As much as saying that kills me, exposing my coward-ness, weakness, and selfishness, I must admit it. I must acknowledge how spineless that is for me to abandon my family. At one point, I did.

I'd had enough. Mentally I was exhausted, emotionally confused, intimately neglected, and spiritually depleted. I had come to the end of my rope. One evening I told my wife I was moving out, then I called my two young daughters along with my wife to the living room and let them know that daddy was moving out for a while. It was the hardest thing I have ever done. A part of me was hoping my wife would try and convince me to stay, "that didn't happen." In my own twisted mind I think I was trying to get her to see it was her fault... what an idiot! Later that evening I went to the movies to try and put this aching feeling of "What have you done" out of my mind; it was as if an anchor of a ship dropped on my heart, I could barely breathe. I don't remember what movie it was but at that moment everything was a haze; I was probably still in shock from the palpating incident of telling my family I was leaving. I remember a scene in the movie that made me realize I had just made the worst decision in my life. The hurt, the pain, the overwhelming guilt of my selfish action weighed so heavily upon me; I began to sob quietly but uncontrollably. I had to leave the theater. I eventually gathered up enough courage that evening to tell my wife I changed my mind. She didn't say much. In fact, I can't recall if she said anything at all. I do remember her not speaking to me for a long time. Who could blame her?

We've moved on from that, but our marriage was still far from where God expects it to be. Every single day I pray over our marriage. There are times I have been physically exhausted, crying out to the Lord in prayer for our marriage.

I have fasted for long periods of time, many days without eating. I have sought professional counseling, spoken to other pastors, read multiple books on marriage, etc., but its prayer that has kept us together.

Are we where God wants us to be today? not yet; "Though it tarries, wait!" God, for whatever reason, has chosen to allow us to climb a few more hills, and that's ok. I now realize it's for our good. Had it not been for our trials and tribulations in our marriage I would not be writing this book nor would have change taken place in my inner man, becoming the husband God created me to be!

Because of prayer, there is a rushing stream of courage and hope and optimism in my soul about our marriage. God has lit the lamp in the lighthouse of our marriage, though there are dark cloudy days at times, but I see a beacon of light drawing us and guiding us in the right direction. There are no more doubts in my mind, there are no "what if's" about the future of our marriage. Faith helps me to see the future even if the present can be unpleasant at times. *"We must see those things that are not as though they were."* My version, "You must see it before you see it." That will preach by the way. You have my permission to use it.

Upon writing this book, I realized that God is pouring my wife and me out as a drink offering. Our trials, tribulations, and suffering are not only for our growth but also for the benefit of those with

similar issues. To be an example to others and encourage them to hang in there until God pulls you through.

One of the books that helped the most while waiting on God in our marriage and allowed me to see MY faults in the marriage was,[31]The Power of a Praying Husband by Stormie Omartian. Brothers and Sisters, this book changed my life! It exposed me to all my ignorance, foolishness, selfishness, idiotic thoughts, sexism, and most of all and more importantly, where I fell short as a man of God, husband, and spiritual leader for my wife and children. Her book hit me over the head with a velvet hammer. Man, what an eye-opener. Husbands get the book! If you don't you are an idiot and don't want to save your marriage anyway. I don't remember why I chose her book but as I was walking down the aisle of a Christian bookstore and out of the hundreds of other books, it caught my attention, "The Power of a Praying Husband." It was a dark time in our marriage and I was looking for any help to guide me out of the darkness. Now, I know, it was the Holy Spirit that led me to her book that day because it has had a profound effect on my life. Although my marriage is still being transformed by the renewing of our mind. Stormie's book helped me to see my wife in a different light through the eyes of a woman, and I'm eternally grateful.

In her opening chapter, she writes, *"Thank you sir, for reading this book. I'm sure that no one is holding a gun to your head to make you do it, but if she is, tell her to put it down because you intend to keep going."* I thought that was clever!

We all have thought our spouse must first change for our marriage to succeed. But that's not how God works; the world works that way but not God. When Jesus met the woman at the well, in (John 4:4-42), who had five husbands and the one she was living with was not married to her; there was one constant in all her relationships, her. We are so easy to blame the other when mostly we are the problem. That was the case in our marriage; I was the problem. My wife, Faith, is the most caring person I

[31] Stormie Omartian, *The Power of a Praying Husband*, Harvey House Publishers, 2001

know. She has a gift of empathy and compassion for people. In our early part of marriage she was vibrant full of anticipation about our family, her career, ready to have a happy life; but she married me. I don't say that with contempt about myself, but recognizing, because of my egocentric ways I damaged her dreams.

She graduated from the University of Texas with a degree in BroadCast Journalism. Faith is highly intelligent and had her own radio talk show at a local radio station. It was an experimental spot that aired around 4 am, but it had potential. I was a Retail Shoe store manager making about 40k at the time and moving up the company ladder. During this time I was offered to manage the second largest store in our company in Houston. It would be a good career move and promotion. Faith made half my salary, so I thought it no big deal to move. It never occurred; it would be an issue. After all, I am the man and the head of the home; I make the decisions for us. You can probably guess where this is going. I do have one excuse, I had not given my life to Jesus then, but still, what a jerk. I told Faith about the opportunity and that we were moving to Houston. I don't recall ever asking her thoughts on the situation but I do remember some push back and reluctance about the move.

Nevertheless, she packed up, left her new career, and headed to Houston to be a shoe manager's wife. Just now, writing this, a horror and a sorrow foster in my heart. How could I do that? How could I give no credence to her feelings and emotions? I believe, and perhaps it's not true, but I believe that was the beginning of our troubled marriage. I don't think Faith has fully ever forgiven me for that stunt; perhaps she has, she says she has, but I don't know?

I have made so many bonehead decisions like that in our marriage and with each one it has damaged our relationship and my beautiful wife who has tolerated each absurdity. And I have the audacity to ask God to change her. "Lord, please forgive me for my sin."

In retrospect, although it has been unpleasant and hurtful to see my wife unhappy, it has caused me to seek God more than ever. I'm still seeking God through prayer while He is changing my heart toward my wife and making me a better man. Prayer does that; you can't honestly and sincerely pray to God and not be changed. Prayer is the instrument of change, "prayer changes things," as they say in the church.

[32]Stormie writes, "When you pray for your wife, you are inviting God to exercise His power in her life. Your prayer enables her to better hear God's voice and respond to God's leading."

Uhm, that sounds good, but is that true? As I meditated on that thought, the Holy Spirit brought to my remembrance (1 Cor. 11:3), *"But I want you to know that the head of every man is Christ, the head of woman is man, and the head of Christ is God."*

If Christ is my head, and He prayed for me, that I might become one with Him, as He did in (John 17:20-26), then as head of my wife I can pray the same prayer, thereby preparing her to be led by God to become one with me. Hallelujah! I'm preaching myself happy!

In the proceeding verses of (1 Cor. 11:4-12), scripture speaks of a covering. I believe and discuss in greater detail in another chapter, that the husband has authority to cover his wife with prayer and God's word. Of course, this does not mean a wife should be dependent on her husband to pray for her, she has as much right to the Saviors throne as her husband to pray for her own deliverance thereby helping her husband become what God intends him to be.

Perhaps I haven't given her a safe place to discuss her beliefs with me and that makes it difficult to pray together. Sometimes I can be overbearing and arrogant about the Bible. Not that I am some spiritual guru, more spiritual than anyone else, not that I think of myself more highly than I ought, or do I? After all, I have studied God's word for 20 years now, I have preached for 18 years, pastored for 12 years. Is it possible, I have become insensitive to her? Do I make her feel unlearned or less important in her beliefs as it pertains to God's word? Am I a Bible bully?

---

[32] Stormie Omartian, *The Power of a Praying Husband*, Harvey House Publishers, 2001, p.32

"And whatsoever ye shall ask in my name, that will I do, that the Father may be glorified in the Son. If ye shall ask any thing in my name, I will do it. (John 14:14) KJV

Does God answer all prayers? In one way or the other, that includes "No." Sometimes we pray for things that are not in Jesus' name; we put His name on it, but He didn't authorize it. For instance: perhaps you're having car trouble; that old beat-up 2002 truck is on its last leg, but you are two months behind on rent and don't have the finances to purchase a new or even a previously owned truck. You go to the Lord in prayer for help, the prayer goes like this, "Father, please help me with my finances, I need a truck that is reliable and won't break down. Would You please open up a door for me to get another vehicle, in Jesus' name?" Then, you get off your knees expecting God to move on your request. You are so sure He is going to answer your prayer; after all, it is in Jesus' name! So, you drive by the dealership and see a 2017 pre owned Ford-F150 in just the right color. You know you can't afford it, but you prayed in Jesus' name. You go on a test drive, and the ether of the experience blinds your mind to all rational thought. You apply for the loan and are turned down. But it is in Jesus' name; you've named it and claimed it, so you head to a dealership that will give anyone a loan at an interest rate of 23% on a $30,000.00 vehicle. You think to yourself, "I will pay it off early." Thereby justifying this stupid decision. You leave the dealership with keys in hand because despite you being behind on your mortgage, you tell yourself God opened a door for you to drive home in your new truck. You go to church, park where everyone can see it because you want to give God the glory, in Jesus' name!

Now you have a car note as much as your mortgage, and you believe because you put Jesus' name on it all will be alright... No, it won't! Jesus is not in the business of His children being in unnecessary debt, and He doesn't approve of people stamping His name to something unreasonable and unrealistic.

Are there Unrealistic Expectations of Prayer? [33]R.C. Sproul writes: "Sometimes we all feel as if our prayers lack the power to penetrate our ceilings. It seems as though our petitions fall on deaf ears and God remains unmoved or unconcerned about our passionate pleading. Why do these feelings haunt us? Prayer is not magic. God is not a celestial bellhop at our beck and call to satisfy our every whim." "In some cases, our prayers must involve the travail of the soul and agony of heart, such as Jesus experienced in the Garden of Gethsemane. Sometimes young Christians have been bitterly disappointed in "unanswered" prayers, not because God failed to keep His promises, but because well-meaning Christians made promises "for" God."

The Habit of Prayer:

That's the POWER of prayer, "habit," No weapon formed against you shall prosper if you are a man or woman of habitual prayer. Along with trials comes the burden of proof you have faith enough to see it through. Along with the heartache comes the transformation of a heart of stone into a heart of flesh. Along with longsuffering, comes perseverance, which produces character, and character hope. That is every Christian's appointment, to persevere, especially in marriage. It is our appointment, our mandate to overcome the challenges. The devil is a magician in making things seem worse than what they really are. Never forget, you already have the VICTORY.

When you can understand, when it is fused to your soul, when you know "That all things work together for good to those who love God, to those who are called according to His purpose." (Rom. 8:28); when your life is so crocheted with this verse, nothing will thwart you from hanging in there until you get the desired results. That's the power of prayer. Much PRAYER much POWER, little prayer, little power.

---

33 R.C. Sproul, *Are there Unrealistic Expectations of Prayer, Eric T Young, Reformed Bibliophile,* June 3, 2010, February 2020

Prayer produces a Christ-like character: Prayer governs and produces integrity. If our conduct is continually sinful much prayer will availeth little. Conduct and character must be wholesome. Righteousness must have prominence in the believer's life. Wicked character is the low ceiling to prayer. It is a strange fire that insults God. How can God answer prayer for your wife to change when adultery is in your bedroom? Jesus says *hypocrite, pull out the tree trunk out of your own eye before you take out the toothpick from someone else's eye-* my translation of (Matthew 7:3).

Adultery might not be your transgression, what about porn, or even flirtation. Jesus says if you lusted in the thought, you've committed it already (Matthew 5:28). What about rudeness to your spouse or abrasive and abusive language? What about ignoring your wife or dodging your responsibility as a father or provider?

There are several things that we should not let the sun go down on besides anger. Sin stifles prayer. However, prayer changes the conduct of men, pureness to their heart is birth in prayer. One cannot come before a Holy God and be unholy; unless he has a contrite heart, or in Christ who make us holy, you have been made righteous through the blood of Lamb and the work of the Holy Spirit, not of your own works. For holy and unholy are not compatible, what does darkness have in common with light. You are unequally yoked with God if you are not in Christ and ongoing "practicing" sin is continually in your life. The Bible says those that practice such things WILL NOT inherit the kingdom of God (Galatians 5:21; 1Corintians 6:9-10; Romans 1:18-32).

I would advise you not to read these scriptures, if you don't want to give up sin truly. Perhaps you can claim ignorance, but once you have seen the word for yourself you will be held accountable before God. A repentant heart must be set before God (Psalm 51:16,17) says, "*For You do not desire sacrifice, or else I would give it: You do not delight in burnt offering. The sacrifices of God are a broken spirit, a broken and contrite heart, these, O God, You will not despise.*"

I had to learn to come to God in prayer with a broken heart for the way I've treated my wife and others. She has not been treated like a butterfly, but a caterpillar. I was unable to see her real beauty. Her concerns, her emotions, were wrapped up and hidden from my sight. Not because she hid them but because I refuse to see them. Thank be to God for (1 John 1: 8,9) *"If we say that we have no sin, we deceive ourselves, and the truth is not in us. If we confess our sins, He is faithful and just to forgive us our sins and to cleanse us from [all] unrighteousness."* Hallelujah, I feel like preaching!

Even if sin is not a practice in your life, coming to God in humility is the access and the key to God hearing our prayer. (1 Peter 5:6) *"Therefore humble yourselves under the mighty hand of God, that He may exalt you in due time."* Prayer is our third eye; it sees things the physical eyes cannot. Prayer sees the past, present, and future. It sees beyond this world into the spiritual world, for all things are first before God in the Spirit at one moment, in the twinkling of an eye. God can see from eternity to eternity in one second. We are bound by time and space; God is not; time and space came forth from God, they are His tools and He uses them as a skilled carpenter uses his. Prayer gives us access to God's tools, it helps build up hope and tear down doubt.

On the way back from the ranch and heading home, after three days of intense prayer and meditation, God gave me an illumination of His word. I realized while driving down a long lonely back road, "The only way to defeat the devil, is, you must defeat him in the spiritual realm before you can have victory in the physical realm." I have read and studied, "For we wrestle not against flesh and blood, but against principalities, against powers, against the rulers of the darkness of this world, against spiritual wickedness in high places," (Ephesians 6:12), but for whatever reason, when God spoke it to my spirit a light was turned on in my mind. It was an illumination to an old word, a fresh oil, a fresh anointing of knowledge and power to defeat Satan.

Spiritual wickedness in high places: We spend so much time, with little gain, fighting each other in the flesh when real victory, the actual defeat of the enemy can only be attained by prayer. When Jesus told Peter, in (Luke 22:31,32), *"The devil wants to sift you like wheat, but I prayed for you, that your faith fails not;"*

My God, my God, what a remarkable response to the enemy's roar. Prayer! Jesus was no novice when it came to tangle with Satan. Before Jesus's birth Satan was out to steal, kill, and destroy the works of Jesus. According to the gospel of Matthew, Mark, and Luke, upon starting His ministry, Jesus had just fasted and prayed for 40 days and 40 nights in the Judean desert; and Satan came with a full force of arsenal, with the highest temptation he could offer, with an offer no man could refuse, save Jesus. Why didn't He give into the temptation? I believe, because He had anointed Himself with prayer as Aaron anointed his head with oil, saturated Himself in prayer, soaked and drenched His spirit in prayer. His body was weak, hungry, exhausted from the heat of the desert, dehydrated and perhaps still shaking from the freezing temperatures of night and weary of wild animals. At His weakest point physically, we could say, He was at His strongest spiritually, because of prayer.

The other example of the POWER of prayer can be found in (Luke 22:44), where Jesus is kneeling down in anguish, the intensity of His prayer was such that He sweat drops of blood; while His disciple couldn't stay awake. Jesus prayed, "Take this cup from Me;" This is one prayer the Father does not answer and I'm glad He didn't. Some Prayers the Lord doesn't answer because we already know the answer. It is those that have learned to walk by faith that need not prayer answered at every request, for they have matured to find the answer and solution within themselves, through His word, and their experiences with God. They've come to know, "Not my will, but thine oh LORD!

Jesus is on the way to the cross to take on the sins of the world, the blackest of darkness of sins. Till this point Jesus is pure light, He is the light, the actual light of God the Father. No darkness has ever tried to enter His being, no sin has ever entered His mind, and now in His darkest hour as it were, Jesus prays, *"If it be thy will, let this cup pass from Me?"* It was prayer that lifted Jesus onto the cross, it was prayer that kept Him on it, and it was prayer that took Him off it, *"Father, into Your hands I commend My Spirit." (Luke 23:46)*

Chapter Twenty-One
PEACE IN MARRIAGE

In her devotional[34] Rebecca Vandoodewaard, says "Do you remember Mr. and Mrs. Hurst *from Pride and prejudice?* She's Mr. Bingley's sister, and she spends most of her time playing cards, the piano, and social games. He spends most of his time drinking and sleeping. Their peaceful marriage is striking: there's no conflict, no hostility. They have a very modern marriage- both partners live their own parallel lives. Peaceful marriages are not as rare as we might think."

This was intriguing: as I understand her article, what seems to be a dysfunction can become functional and bring about a feeling of peace in the marriage. If a husband and wife carry out their own interests and desires independent of each other, a certain amount of peace can be attained. If finances are not necessarily a concern and overt pressures of life are not frequent, and both are pursuing their own goals and are free to do their own thing without having to commit or depend on each other, this can create a kind of peace. However, it's certainly not the peace that surpasses all understanding; it is not the peace of God but of convenient circumstance. Once affliction, calamity, or tribulation come, and they are forced to engage in the sacrifice of their own

[34] Rebecca Vandoodewaard, *Reformation Women: Sixteen-Century Figures Who Shaped Christianity's Rebirth,* Heritage Books, 2017

interests and pursuits, the counterfeit peace they have will crumble under pressure.

She writes, "A marriage can be peaceful if one spouse decides to sacrifice him- or herself for peace. It might be a wife suffering silently through the husbands' neglect, porn addiction, or emotional abuse. It could be a husband living on a proverbial roof-top (Prov. 21:9), working to deal with credit card debt, or keeping His head down through nagging comparisons."

I'm inclined to agree; there are examples all around us that support this false notion of peace. I know many couples that live separate lives in their homes, and only when it is beneficial or necessary do they come together, because it is financially or paternally better or convenient to stay married, they manufacture a life within the marriage that brings compromise to masquerade as peace. Peace with error is not peace!

She also writes, "The measure of marriage is not the level of peace in the relationship; it's the source and goal of that peace."

Bullseye! Christ is our peace, He is the Prince of Peace, He has sent us His peace in the form of the Holy Spirit. He is our source of and for all comfort. Peace cannot come when both spouses have conspired to live their own lives apart from Him, it is then a life of sin, and misery loves company.

In (Romans 1:28-32) Paul writes, *"28 Since they thought it foolish to acknowledge God, he abandoned them to their foolish thinking and let them do things that should never be done. 29 Their lives became full of every kind of wickedness, sin, greed, hate, envy, murder, quarreling, deception, malicious behavior, and gossip. 30 They are backstabbers, haters of God, insolent, proud, and boastful. They invent new ways of sinning, and they disobey their parents. 31 They refuse to understand, break their promises, are heartless, and have no mercy. 32 They know God's justice requires that those who do these things deserve to die, yet they do them anyway. Worse yet, they encourage others to do them, too." NLT.*

There is an old parable that says crabs in the bucket keep other crabs in the bucket; when one is just about to reach the top and climb out another crab will catch it by the leg and pull it back into the bucket. Does your marriage feel that way at times?

But a healthy Christian marriage isn't supposed to be that way, we are to encourage each other to excel, to achieve their highest potential and if they can't reach the top of the bucket together, the other reaches back down and pull up their spouse and they come out together. A Christian marriage should be peaceful but that doesn't mean there won't be disagreements or different thoughts about a matter; even confrontation can be positive when done with love. To have true peace in marriage, both husband and wife must first be restored, then reconciled. They must be built back up in Christ individually then reconciliation with each other will happen naturally. There is no genuine reconciliation without genuine restoration of past pain and hurt, through Christ Jesus. Secure in their relationship with Him, they can be vulnerable and forgiving with each other which will, in time, produce a meaningful healthy, and peaceful marriage.

But what if your spouse is hurtful, harmful, and infidelity or porn, deception etc. is a continued problem. Should a wife remain in that situation for the sake of false peace? Do you have the right to seperate, are there biblical principles or scripture to support separation until reconciliation has occurred? I believe there are. Some churches teach that separation is not biblical; I disagree. We know that infidelity can be a reason for getting divorced according to Jesus, however, what if infidelity hasn't occurred, but emotional, physical, or sexual abuse has happened and the wife wants to remain married but seperates until Christ-like change has taken place in her husband? I think scripture supports separation in those cases: in 1 Corinthians 7:10 where Paul writes, "To the married I give this charge (not I, but the Lord): The wife should not separate from her husband (but if she does, she should remain unmarried or else be reconciled to her husband), and the husband should not divorce his wife." ESV

Separation is not the preferred choice, but if it happens, she is to remain unmarried. I believe it is vidal that a wife, or husband not stay in an abusive relationship, but I'm not automatically expressing divorce either. Other scripture I believe supports separation: Proverbs 14:7 – "Leave the presence of a fool, for there you do not meet words of knowledge." 2 Thessalonians 3:6, 2 Timothy 3:1-5, Proverbs 22:24-25; I know these might seem broad but I think they hold merit in the case of domestic abuse.

Chapter Twenty-Two

JESUS DEMANDS ALLEGIANCE

For which of you, intending to build a tower, does not sit down first and count the cost, whether he has enough to finish it- Luke 14:28

And Jesus said unto him, No man, having put his hand to the plough, and looking back, is fit for the kingdom of God.- Luke 9:62 KJV

Balancing Family and Ministry come with a cost: strangely, the Bible is somewhat vague and ambiguous about a formula of balancing marriage, family, and ministry, because there isn't one. What I mean is, it does not in a transparent manner, give ABC or 1-2-3 instructions on balancing this widespread issue. Where does it state explicitly that ministry is more of a priority than family, or those called into ministry should make their family their priority? Most would undoubtedly establish the second statement to be the case; family is the primary ministry we have been taught. This problem is a dichotomy and frustrates the people of God and more so, those called into ministry. Guilt is inevitable at some point until one comes to rest in our own consciousness about the matter. I can't say definitively which method. option. or opinion is right or wrong; only rest in my own conclusion through studying God's word and the leading of the Holy Spirit as it pertains to my life and my situation.

I consider the thought process of the apostle Paul at this point when He says *"I, not the Lord,"* giving a command on marriage; or when he gives instruction on eating what is or isn't lawful, depending on one's own conscience (1 Corinthians 7:12; 10:23-33). This is a conclusion each soul must come to the center in their own conscience. If a person after careful study and prayer concludes that their family should take priority over the ministry, then let him be settled in his own mind of the matter. In this case, I believe God is still honored. Likewise, if someone is firmly convinced that ministry at times takes precedence over family or at least alongside family, then let their conscience be to the glory of God. Once again, I believe God will honor him. There are times the Bible is not yes or no, but what pleases the Lord. The point I want to make is, whichever side of the dispute you fall on, it is not sinful.

After speaking with more tenured pastors on their thoughts, most of them express that they don't have easy answers and that they have experienced a lot of frustrations and disappointments as they've tried to sort it out in their homes and churches.

Let's consider the two views on the matter:

Over the last few decades, it has been taught, God, Family, and Church is the balanced order and key to a healthy family dynamic. But is it?

This dilemma is so heavy on the soul it has caused some to give up ministry, while the conflict has so uprooted other's families, broken homes were the result. The problem is you're pulled in two directions; as a pastor, you want to fulfill your calling as a shepherd because sheep need to be attended to. As a father, the sheep at home need to be attended to as well. How to choose or when to choose is complicated, either way brings a double-edge sword that penetrates the deep recesses of the heart, dividing it, but the duty of both are so interconnected that it is as the joint and marrow of the bone. Only God's word can divide between the two. Let's do some cutting with the word of God.

First View- Family First: [35]In his blog Dr. Heath Lambert writes (1 Timothy 3:4-5) *"says that the minister must, "Manage his own household well, with all dignity keeping his children submissive, for if someone does not know how to manage his own household, how will he care for God's church?"*

He writes, "The simple truth of this passage is that men are not allowed to care for God's church until they have learned to care for their own home. There can be no success in caring for God's church until there has been a success in caring for your home. This means that men who are committed to having successful ministries must be committed to having well-ordered homes. You cannot have the former without the latter."

I certainly understand the premise of his assessment, but I'm not inclined to agree wholeheartedly. I know pastors with troubled marriages and dysfunctional families that have huge ministries: have they not cared for God's people in a well-ordered manner? Likewise, there are pastors with a healthy family relationship with a troubled church. I agree it is unlikely that a man with an unsubmissive wife and unruly children will be effective in shepherding God's people long term; that is usually a recipe for failure; more often than not a more profound issue lingers and if not dealt with will cause harm to both the family and church. However, God knows whom He calls into pastoring, does God simply toss His called one aside because their life is out of balance or does He give them the grace to go and grow?

He goes on to say, as I paraphrase- If your children are disobedient and unruly and your wife is feeling neglected then the pastor must spend more time with the family and not the church; if the congregation doesn't like it then we might have to consent to an angry congregation or no congregation rather than a broken home.

---

[35] Heath Lambert, *Balancing family and ministry: Part 1: priority capacity*, Southern Equip, Southern Seminary, June 5, 2014, February 2020

I see his logic and, in some sense, agree, but can we definitively say that's God's will? Is it God's will to let family dictate our calling?

No doubt, Dr. Lambert makes valid points and believes his evaluation of this perplexing problem is accurate; in retrospect, to a degree, so do I. However, when the Lord Jesus calls a person to pastor His Church the outlook on the purpose of life changes. You no longer have one family but two. It's as though God gives the pastor two families to care for.

[36]Barnabas Piper, the son of pastor John Piper, says, "What pastors need to realize is that their first calling is to their families, not the church. Yes, the church is a calling too, and balancing the two is enormously difficult. As in many other industries, the job does sometimes demand attention in a way that cannot be ignored. But when someone marries and becomes a parent, those people—the family—must come first. It is wrong, sinful, to put us on the sidelines and treat pastoral ministry as if it is the 'primary' or 'real' calling. Pastors must keep the dual calls in proper relation to one another, as difficult as that may be." Finally, Piper concludes: "The pastor's family needs the best of his time and energy."

[37]Dr. James Dobson, the retired host of "Focus on the Family" Broadcast, for almost forty years, shaped the way evangelicals see the church family dynamic. Through his own experiences, he taught, God, family, ministry, is the correct Christian alignment. His theology to this day, I believe, is the calibrating instrument that has had the most profound impact on church/ family doctrine. But is that doctrine correct?

---

[36] Barnabas Piper, *The Pastor's Kid: Finding Your Own Faith and Identity*, David C Cook, 2014, chapter 6

[37] Gary Derickson,*Sacrificing Family: Does Jesus' Teaching on Discipleship Invalidate the Modern Emphasis on Family before Ministry?* Dedicated Journal, Corbon School of Ministry, February 18th, 2016, February 2020

The Rebuttal

Second view: [38]Gary Derickson writes, "The now popular idea that one should not neglect family for the sake of ministry is an American cultural value, not a biblical one. A survey of the modern evangelical view of family and ministry reveals its emphasis on not allowing ministry to cause one to fail to meet his or her family's needs. The problems that result from a husband and father's neglect of his wife and children has motivated this emphasis and influenced the interpretation and application of certain biblical passages related to the family. The result has been a hierarchy of commitment: first God, then family, and then church (ministry), even for pastors. However, Jesus' teachings on discipleship conflict- with our modern emphasis."

In his journal, he asserts, Jesus teaches, all who want to follow Jesus must be willing to sacrifice all, including family.

For today's church, that creates a problem and causes leadership to water down their commitment to their church responsibilities. Our churches have taught God, family, church, it's been driven into the psyche this is the formula to a balanced life. Derickerson, says, as a result, *"The weakened church has subsequently lost its willingness to do those things necessary to reach the lost world around it with the gospel."*

He asks the question, "Can we follow Christ the way He wants us to and still preserve our families?" Great question, it's the central focus of this book, "Can we? If so, how? Through the teachings of the Bible I believe it is possible, but even if it is not achieved, serving the Lord can never be wrong, we might do it the wrong way but serving Him is what we are called to first. With that said, "Church" has changed, not the body of Christ but how the body functions in today's culture. With new inventions of technology, the course of this world is moving at a rapid pace but decelerates the personal human interaction element. We

---

[38] Gary Derickson,*Sacrificing Family: Does Jesus' Teaching on Discipleship Invalidate the Modern Emphasis on Family before Ministry?* Dedicated Journal, Corbon School of Ministry, February 18th, 2016, February 2020

would rather interact through our technology even at home. The father is on his laptop in his office, the mother is on Facebook in the bedroom, the children are chatting on… whatever!, in their rooms, and once addicted to this trance, it becomes more difficult to motivate parishioners to assemble locally at church. Larger ministries can absorb missing in action members, but it can have a depressing effect on ministries with membership under a hundred people. It is not church that causes imbalance, family can be neglected while at home.

What does Jesus Teach? Is His teaching heriticle to Church culture?

[39]Francis and Lisa Chan reject this mindset. "We all have callings from God, and those callings are bigger than our marriages. Seeking His kingdom must be our first priority, and if we're not careful, marriage can get in the way. … Can you really call your marriage 'good' if your focus on your family keeps you from making disciples, caring for the poor, reaching out to the lost, and using your talents and resources for others?" Paul seems to agree that marriage can get in the way of fully giving yourself to God. According to 1 Corinthians 7:32-35 New American Standard Bible (NASB), Paul writes…

32 *"But I want you to be free from concern. One who is unmarried is concerned about the things of the Lord, how he may please the Lord;* 33 *but one who is married is concerned about the things of the world, how he may please his wife,* 34 *and his interests are divided. The woman who is unmarried, and the virgin, is concerned about the things of the Lord, that she may be holy both in body and spirit; but one who is married is concerned about the things of the world, how she may please her husband.* 35 *This I*

[39] Gary Derickson,*Sacrificing Family: Does Jesus' Teaching on Discipleship Invalidate the Modern Emphasis on Family before Ministry?*, Dedicated Journal, Corbon School of Ministry, February 18th, 2016, February 2020

say for- your own benefit; not to put a restraint upon you, but [a] *to promote what is appropriate and to secure undistracted devotion to the Lord."*

It is clear that lines have been drawn, at least by some. But how does one answer the question of commitment to the church or to the family? Let's begin by looking at what Jesus says.

What does Jesus think:

How did Jesus treat his family? What did He prioritize? If we were to evaluate honestly how Jesus interacted with His earthly family compared with His church family, most would be put off by His choices. That is not a popular statement these days, but are we to conclude it is wrong automatically? When truthful with ourselves and the interpretation of scripture, it is hard to ignore the fact that Jesus holds no punches when it comes to loyalty to Him verses our families. He clearly teaches that following Him "in ministry" is of greater importance. However, I'm not totally convinced Jesus is not making a more significant point, to show how far we are from loving God with all our heart, mind, and strength; no one can do that, and yet, He is still merciful and gracious toward us. This does not negate the fact we are to press toward that mark daily, trying to apprehend it fully.

To illustrate Jesus' radical teaching, let's take Luke's gospel into account (Luke 14:25-33). Keep in mind Jesus is speaking to a people and culture that puts family loyalty above all else. Did Jesus bring division in families? Yes. Why? Because in His kingdom that is at hand all commitment must be to the King of the kingdom. He must have complete reign in our lives, which subjugates the family to a lesser love. When the King calls all other responsibilities are put on hold, they are sacrificed until the call is complete. There is a cost in following Christ, and, at times, it will cost time with ministry or family. I am not saying a person should divorce and leave their family for the sake of ministry. I am saying, according to the teaching of Jesus, His body, "the church" which is His ministry must be paramount; that seems a ridiculous even blasphemous assertion, and yet, truth is evident in it.

For example, (Luke 14:25-33)

“[25] Now great crowds accompanied him, and he turned and said to them, [26] “If anyone comes to me and does not hate his own father and mother and wife and children and brothers and sisters, yes, and even his own life, he cannot be my disciple. [27] Whoever does not bear his own cross and come after me cannot be my disciple. [28] For which of you, desiring to build a tower, does not first sit down and count the cost, whether he has enough to complete it? [29] Otherwise, when he has laid a foundation and is not able to finish, all who see it begin to mock him, [30] saying, ‘This man began to build and was not able to finish.’ [31] Or what king, going out to encounter another king in war, will not sit down first and deliberate whether he is able with ten thousand to meet him who comes against him with twenty thousand? [32] And if not, while the other is yet a great way off, he sends a delegation and asks for terms of peace. [33] So therefore, any one of you who does not renounce all that he has cannot be my disciple.” ESV version.

These words of Jesus are hard. Hard to understand and accept. We tend to take difficult scriptures like these and make them hypothetical to ease our conscience and to soften the blow. However, Jesus’ words are not hypothetical. ***His demand for loyalty is absolute.***

Devotion to family is a human and Christian duty but is never supreme if that duty to God is compromised.

Gary Dickerson writes in the same journal, “Jesus speaks to them in terms of willingness to die for Him. Anyone unwilling could not be His disciple. However, what He says about family is not a question of willingness, but an expectation. Jesus uses the verb for “hate” to contrast their loyalty for Him with their love for family members, and even for their own lives. For Jesus, it is not a question of degrees, but of opposites. One may argue that Jesus is speaking in absolutes that He knows are impossible, using hyperbole, and so not to be understood or applied literally. However, the point He makes has to do with levels of commitment. *Hate* is used to communicate the idea that they are to "esteem" their family members *less* than they esteem Jesus."

In (Luke 9:60-61), we clearly see Jesus's command to follow Him supersedes any other commitment. "[61] *And another also said, Lord, I will follow thee; but let me first go bid them farewell, which are at home at my house.*[62] *And Jesus said unto him, No man, having put his hand to the plough, and looking back, is fit for the kingdom of God".*

Also in (Matthew 8:19-22), Jesus makes a statement that in today's society, that would be considered insensitive, thoughtless, inconsiderate, uncaring, unsympathetic, and callous. And even though we may not say it out loud or in the presence of other Christians, it is precisely what we think. How can Jesus be so cold to this man who only wants to bury his dad first, before he commits to Jesus's ministry? But let's not skip over the scribe who says He wanted to follow Jesus *"wherever you go."* Although we are called into ministry, we should nevertheless count the cost; because sometimes where the Lord takes us, we might not want to follow.

In both cases, Jesus wants them to consider what they will sacrifice. Jesus is not restrained with his word, and He does not sugarcoat what He says, He doesn't hold back the shock and awe of His command, He is untethered to the demands of social and emotional correctness. This disciple did not make an outlandish request by any means. In the Jewish culture, it was the son's obligation to bury his father according to (Lev 21:1-2).

[29] So Jesus answered and said, "Assuredly, I say to you, there is no one who has left house or brothers or sisters or father or mother or wife or children or lands, for My sake and the gospel's, [30] who shall not receive a hundredfold now in this time—houses and brothers and sisters and mothers and children and lands, with persecutions—and in the age to come, eternal life. [31] But many who are first will be last, and the last first."

Again, it is difficult to turn our minds over to such an unnatural way of thinking and living, but Jesus's followers must go beyond the natural to the spiritual way of life, for they live in a different kingdom. They must go the extra mile giving up their garment of domestic care, and their coat too, if required by Jesus. These men wanted to follow Jesus but felt the burden of their obligations to their families. They had been taught all their lives; not providing for their family is worse than an infidel. Maybe their motives are that innocent, but it does not change the fact, Jesus was not their priority no matter how much they said they wanted to follow Him.

What about Jesus' family? Did Jesus walk the talk? In (Matthew 12:46-50) *"[46] While He was still talking to the multitudes, behold, His mother and brothers stood outside, seeking to speak with Him. [47] Then one said to Him, "Look, Your mother and Your brothers are standing outside, seeking to speak with You." [48] But He answered and said to the one who told Him, "Who is My mother and who are My brothers?" [49] And He stretched out His hand toward His disciples and said, "Here are My mother and- My brothers![50] For whoever does the will of My Father in heaven is My brother and sister and mother."*

What are we to do with this text? Should we set it aside as hyperbole? Should we see the greater meaning while dismissing its basic statement? How far are we willing to travel down this road of sacrifice? Will God be angry if we forsake all for Christ? Will He consider us infidels if we drop our nets "responsibilities" and become fishers of men?

The reality is, Jesus is the eldest; it was His responsibility to look after His mother and family, and yet, He prioritizes His domestic obligations to attend to His heavenly duties. No doubt they think He is mad, lost His mind, but His "mind" was faced toward Jerusalem like a flint.

It's as though Jesus places higher importance on those doing the will of His Father than those that are not, not that His mother wasn't in the will of God, obviously she was, but she is now a part of Jesus' spiritual family.

But *"He stretched out His hands toward His disciples,"* that is key! His disciples are His family; this is where I think most of us miss it. If my wife and children are disciples of Jesus, and though they might not follow in the responsibility of shepherding the flock, they do have the responsibility to sacrifice to some degree for the flock, because the congregation is family.

So, what price do the families of the apostles pay while they "leave all" to follow Jesus? There is a price. They had to leave house and home and perhaps they returned in the evening; nevertheless, most of their time was occupied with Jesus. They walked away from a career and income for ministry. Following Jesus clearly supersedes familial obligations along with every other commitment one might have in life. All of Jesus' disciples had to "neglect" their families to some degree.

Uneasy as that is to say, ultimately, we must too, at least at times, if that is what it takes to fulfill a responsibility He has given us. But I believe there can be a balance, not perfectly, but a balance that is different for each of us. What I can or cannot balance may be different from the man across the street. Life is not bottled up nice and neat, the variations of life are so diverse only God has a perfectly balanced scale. I believe God gives us the flexibility to prioritize as needed. As stated in an earlier chapter, I had certainly put church ahead of my wife and family in a selfish way.

Right or wrong, I believed I was in the will of the Lord. Was my neglect of family the cause of the chaos in our marriage? I'm sure it was, but even if the role were reversed and I spent more time with family than attending my responsibilities at church, would chaos be absent from our marriage? I doubt it! The church may have brought our problems to the surface, but it wasn't the cause. The actual reason was selfishness. I was selfish in thinking my call was more important and gave me a license to treat my wife and family with reckless neglect and abandonment. Until my wife and I came to grips with our own faults it didn't matter what the effect was, the cause would remain immersed waiting to rise up and make itself known regardless of the trial.

What about the husband's role in marriage as written in (Ephesians 5:25-33)? Can a man love the church as much as he loves his wife? Put another way, how can a husband love his wife sacrificially and still serve and obey Christ unconditionally? Some teach to neglect the family to serve God is wrong, even sin. Is it fair to make us choose, surely, God would not put us in those situations?

But He does! Every day I have to choose whom I will serve, my domestic responsibilities, or my pastoral commitments. As for me and my house, we will serve the Lord! It has not been easy, and we still have difficult discussions about what is important and what is not. I navigate through it with one thought in mind: "*Does it please God?*" Everything is measured by that, every decision, act or deed, should be guided by *does it please God?*

If this is the mindset, the choice will always be right, even if it appears to have a negative effect on those around you. Also, if finances are cut in half by a decision to take lesser pay or leave a secular career to go into ministry, no doubt a family sacrifice is made. But if we seek God's kingdom and His righteousness first, all our needs will be met. We may not eat steak every night, but pork n beans and weenies will fill you up just the same. You might not drive a Mercedes, but a Hyundai will travel the same road.

The call of His under-shepherd is for His flock. When one of Jesus' sheep needs a shepherd's care, He expects His under-shepherd to meet those needs immediately. He is Jesus' physical comforting presence in that moment of *legitimate* need. I say legitimate because the sheep tend to take advantage of the shepherd, so we must have discernment. That church member has emotional and spiritual needs that Jesus wants to be met then, not after the "big game" is over or when it is convenient for the pastor and his family. And, yes, that does mean leaving the family and going to the person who needs comfort and encouragement. However, Jesus expects the shepherd to meet the requirement of his personal home as well. The Ministry does not give us a pass on these responsibilities. But the family must be taught the order of responsibility. I have failed in so many ways in this. I have not taught my family the divine order, I expected them just to fall in line with it, what a colossal mistake.

The Bible is full of examples of people sacrificing family when they hear the voice of God. I can't deny the story of Abraham and his son. Even though God knew He would not let Abraham sacrifice his son, Abraham didn't know that. Abraham was ready not only to sacrifice his son, but his future promise of inheritance as well, and at the same time, he knew God would somehow keep His promise. Over and over again are examples of God's people sacrificing their family duties for their call. This does not mean men are not responsible for their families. They are and God will hold us accountable, but He will always give us the grace to do both.

Sometimes, perhaps most times, spouses and families are not willing to sacrifice as much for the church as the pastor does. After all, he is the one called! Pastor's families need him too, and their needs are real. They have volleyball games, school events, and family night on Fridays. Is it fair to expect them to be as dedicated as their dad, the pastor? I don't think so, and that's being real. At the same time, God knows the sacrifice and He knows your labor in the Lord is not in vain.

Conclusion of the Matter

So, what is the answer? Here are my thoughts: Faith and I are still working through our differences; however, since the start of this book until its last chapter our relationship has substantially improved. Through much prayer and fasting, exhaustively studying, wise counsel, and self-examination of my own failures, I have come to realize the power to change our circumstances is within us. I began to see my wife and our struggles through the eyes of God and realized, although heavy on our shoulders, it was but a feather on God's. When I realized God was not specifically concerned about the technique or even the commitment to both marriage and ministry, but the daily bread He supplied each day, and to see Him in every important decision.

In other words, do not be concerned about tomorrow, for tomorrow has its own concern. But rely on His Holy Spirit to lead and guide you with each decision day by day; to feed me that day with the right choice. When I got this revelation, it freed me from trying to choose what was more crucial, ministry or family. I believe that's a battle you can't win and Satan will use ambiguity to cause guilt and confusion. I have learned to let each day bring its own challenges and adjust my decisions based on what is most important at the moment.

For example, if I promised my daughter, I would come to her final track meet of the year, but on the way, I get a call that one of our members was in a car accident and rushed to the hospital. What should I do? Usually, I would attend to the flock and possibly break my daughter's heart. But now, I pray that the Lord will give me guidance to make the right choice, and if He leads me to the track meet the member will have to wait. If He leads me to the hospital, my daughter will have to miss me at the track meet. Although disappointment can come with either choice made, I won't have guilt because the Holy Spirit has directed my actions. Moreover, I believe the Lord will place forgiveness in the heart of whoever might have been disappointed by my decision.

If I have raised my children to understand sometimes dad might miss the track meet because, at times, I must sacrifice the joy and memory of seeing her compete to help someone in need. She will come to understand that God requires all of us to sacrifice sometimes and it will be a life lesson that carries her through life's difficult times. No verse tells me when I'm traveling on the road too much and neglecting my family or the exact amount of time to spend with my wife or children, or the flock of God for that matter. In fact, the Bible doesn't make a distinction between work and life and religion because, in the ancient world, work-life and family life were often integrated. Families worked together in their family trade. Jesus probably didn't have to leave the house to do his carpentry with Joseph; they likely worked together within their own home. I think about why some pastors are not combining their families with the ministry. Should it not be a family affair? If you believe that God called you into ministry and not your wife or children, you would be right; but He does call them to be involved and connected in the ministry. If we could take advantage of the opportunities where and when the family could co-labor and assist in ministry, we would spend more time together and less time apart.

Chapter Twenty-Three

DEFICIENCIES AND FRAILTIES

"Behold, I was brought forth in iniquity, and in sin did my mother conceive me." (Psalm 51:5) ESV.

It is August 1942, a blisteringly hot summer afternoon in central Texas. An old man is sitting on an old rocking chair on the porch of a two-bedroom shotgun house with outside latrines. It is without central or portable air conditioning and the old man seemed to have resigned to the fact there is no escape from the heat. He has a despondent stare as if he is in another place and time. The locals walk by, aware of the old man but he is just another feature of the landscape, not even a shout, "Hi, Mr. Brown." Sweat drips passed his gray eyebrows and down the side of his wrinkled face, and the only thing keeping him from slipping out of the chair is his hunched back, leaning him forward and a reflection down memory lane. He remembers his past; a time he wishes could be erased from his mind. He has committed horrible, awful things that seem to some degree, justify his current misery.

He is broke, not able to pay the electric bill, he is an alcoholic, not sure where his next drink will come from. With smoked filled lungs and cirrhosis of the liver from alcohol poisoning, his health is depleting, and his body is breaking down. A small statured man standing about 5'5 and looks like the 40s actor Edward G. Robinson. He is my grandfather, and this is as far back as the story goes about my ancestry on my mother's side. Not too much is known about our great-great-grandfather and great-great-grandmother, other than his name was Mr. Willis, a white man, a doctor who owned slaves. He was fond of one particular female slave, apparently, in many ways. She is my great-great-grandmother, a dark black woman with big hands and feet; I am told by my older brother who found an old photo in the public library in Coleman, Texas. She had daughters by Mr. Willis; one of those daughters married a half Negro and Mexican man named Cece Brown. This is the old man on the porch; uneducated and could barely speak English. The rumor is he shot and killed a couple of men, molested his four daughters and possibly his two sons. They were beautiful daughters and the talk of this small town, and popular with the men. And some say the sons were just as good looking as the girls.

I am told our family was the poorest of the poor, if not the poorest. My mother and siblings were raised in an unstable abusive environment. They were scarred psychologically and emotionally, and all grew up with some sort of addiction; sexual, alcohol, drugs; one of the boys was a homosexual, and the girls just seem to always make the wrong choice in men. I now understand why my mother rarely smiled, if ever. I can't find any pictures of her smiling. She was a broken woman by the time I was born, the last of nine children. Though my father has remained married to her since he was 18 and she 16, as you would imagine, they had a volatile marriage.

To my knowledge, they never physically fought, except once that I can remember. My mother threw a plate at my father and it hit him in the forehead, and he was sent to the hospital to get stitches. Mostly, they argued like cats and dogs my father told me.

I know nothing about my father's side of the family, not even his biological father's first name. My dad didn't talk about his family at all. They were an estranged family and not very close, though he had three sisters. His biological father died when he was three months old and his mother remarried to a man who beat my father repeatedly; until one day he told his stepfather he was going to kill him. After that day, his mother was forced to put her son out of the house at 16. The emotional and physiological scars my mother and father had to endure; this kind of childhood is devastating to the human spirit, and an easy target for the forces of darkness. Neither my mother nor father knew the Lord. In fact, my father was an agnostic until right before he died. Not sure if my mother ever accepted Christ before she passed away. These are the demons passed on to my siblings and me. All of us are attached spiritually to our ancestors and to some degree bear our parent's sins, not that we are responsible and judged for their sins, but the residual mental and physiological, and dare I say, spiritual trauma tends to visit the seed of men. Some people would argue this fact, but biblically it is true. From the beginning all men contracted sin through our first father, Adam. It is the father that bears the seed of life and the mother is the incubator and nurturer of that seed.

I make mention of this spiritual truth only to paint a canvas of my own faults, and to seek some perception into why I might nurture certain undesirable traits. Not to excuse my actions or lay blame in my family tree, but to pinpoint behavior from their past that may affect my present.

At the ranch, I'm repenting of my sin. No doubt, we all come into this world full of deficiencies, frailties, weakness, and the propensity bent toward transgression. From our parents Adam and Eve, and grandparents and great-grandparents, and so on, we inherited what is known as a "State of Sin," or nature of sin. We were born into it without any power to have a say-so in the matter. In theology, the term is called "Federalism," meaning we have a federal head "Adam" that activated and initiated a sin nature in all that would come from his seed. "[12] *Therefore, just as through one-man sin entered the world, and death through sin, and thus death spread to all men, because all sinned.*" (Rom 5:12)

As beautiful as a new newborn baby might be, beneath the captivating dark brown eyes and an infectious smile the bundle of joy we hold in our arms is sin-nature and waiting to be shaped. Its desiring to be formed in iniquity, its fashioned and twisted into its preferred choice of sin. Over time, the infant becomes by nature what it is wrought to be. It has not an option; it cannot be what it is not; just as a dog cannot become a cat, a bird cannot become a horse because their nature has fixed, fashioned, and designed them to be what they are. However, I thank God He sent a second Adam, Jesus Christ, and through His Spiritual seed we are born again, born in His righteousness. As stated throughout this book, when God first created man holy and righteous He created them to be in His image to present His character, a reflection of Him to be established on earth.

Sin entered the world through mankind's disobedience, corrupting the blood flow of righteousness, holiness, and the perfect attributes of God in man. According to (Romans 6:6) this infectious venom poisoned and infiltrated humanity through his nature and lived out in flesh and blood. Since there is only one bloodline for humanity, we all incubated and contained the sin of our first father. It would be easy to blame Adam but I would venture to say had it been you and I, we too likely would have tasted the fruit of disobedience. Not because God made us imperfect, but because we have a free will to choose to obey Him or not. For mankind, the only way to be perfect is to have the ability to choose, to choose good or bad, righteousness, or evil. This was the choice God planted in the middle of the Garden of Eden. Without choice, there's no free will, and without free will, there is no perfect being. I Believe this is one reason for the "Tree of the knowledge of good and evil" to activate our free will. Being created perfectly does not mean beyond being corrupted. Satan knew this; if any being was perfect, it was the Archangel Lucifer.

In Ezekiel 28:12-19, we have an accurate picture of Satan. *"You were the seal of perfection, Full of wisdom and perfect in beauty . . . You were the anointed cherub who covers; I established you . . . you were perfect in your ways from the day you were created."* This sounds nothing like the typical image of Satan that many people have. He was an anointed cherub created by God as the highest-ranked angel and in the highest elevated position. What corrupted Lucifer we don't know exactly, but Satan turned his eyes away from his Creator and began to admire the creation; himself. *"You corrupted your wisdom for the sake of your splendor,"* (Ezekiel 28:17) He became proud and exalted himself and desire to rule was born in him. He wished to put himself in God's place.

Put a pin in that last paragraph; we will come back to it. We know pride played its part, but where did pride originate? These questions the Bible doesn't answer and beyond my comprehension. Satan used his knowledge of good and evil to deceive Eve, who then gave the forbidden fruit to Adam, her husband with her. Both perfect but made an imperfect decision, just as Lucifer did. The creature was perfect but gifted with free will. What is free will? **Free will** is the ability to choose between different possible courses of action unimpeded.

It is the power of acting without the constraint of necessity or fate; the ability to work at one's own discretion. Free will is only concerned with do or not do, obey, or not obey. It is neither perfect nor imperfect, but free, free to choose. God has given us great power, the power to choose, to say yes or to say no to God within the umbrella of His sovereignty. The same God that does not give this power to the sun and moon the sky and sea, the earth and fire the wind and all elements of the Universe; even the animals and all created life on earth obey God. They obey Him every second of the day without fail. Only man and woman in this natural world have the gift of free-will. Choice carries the awesome power and responsibility to love or not love God. Free will must have its opportunity to fail, to fall, and choose incorrectly; otherwise, it would be a manufactured unauthentic will, forced to worship God without the ability to express sincere love toward Him. To show God true love is to give God true submission of the will. After the Fall, man lost the ability to obey God and love Him fully. Man became death; anything that is separated from God dies. Disobedience separates us from God and His Spirit would not dwell with man forever. *"In the day you eat of it you will truly die"* was God's warning to Adam. It wasn't the fruit itself that infected Adam and Eve with sin, but their disobedience. When Adam disobeyed God's Law, he broke God's heart. When we break God's law, we break God's heart. And because He is a *just* God, *justice* must be administered, or His heart would forever be broken.

I remember my first broken heart; her name was Louise. It was my sophomore year of high school, and she was the prettiest girl in school. She had wavy black silky hair down to her shoulders; caramel-colored skin so soft and smooth, she always wore the most intoxicating fragrance that smelled so good. Her facial bone structure resembled the features of a Navaho Indian with high cheekbones, pearl white teeth, with a smile so sexy it made all the boys feeble at the knees. Louise was an athlete; she ran track, so her muscle tone and curvy body would have all the boy's jaw drop when she walked by. She lived about a mile from my house; every so often I would walk over to her house because I didn't have a car. We were not affluent and couldn't afford a car for a teenager. Louise and I would sit and talk on her front porch for some time. One day I gathered enough courage to ask her out to the movies.

So, the next day, I rode my friends' bike to her house with quarters in my pocket ready to take Louise to the movies; "it was not a well thought out plan."

The movie theater was quite a distance away. How would we get there? I had a pocket full of quarters and a bike. I was just excited she said yes but didn't think it through...**come on man!** Well, we didn't go to the movies that day. I dropped the ball big time. About a week passed by before I went by her house again, I think I was too embarrassed before. As I approach her front porch, I see my cousin Fred sitting, talking with Louise. They seemed to be having a good time. Fred lived in a town about an hour away named Coleman, the same town near the ranch I spoke about in the first chapter. I didn't even know Fred was in town; I didn't even know Fred knew Louise. I was happy to see Fred; we were close. "What's up Fred, my brother, how are you doing? It's good to see you, man, you gonna come by the house later?" We all talked for a while, but I had to leave soon. I said goodbye to them and went on my way.

A couple of days later I go to see Louise, she's kind of stand-offish and not talking the way she used to when we were so in love, at least I thought we were, I certainly was. She soon informed me not long in our conversation that she is now dating FRED. Taken aback, I didn't know what to say, but I tried to keep my composure and not let her see the damage she had done. I don't remember how I left, or words I used to say goodbye, but I didn't see Louise for a long time after that. I was crushed, my heart had been ripped out. She had broken my law of love, "Do not love Fred over me." I was a recluse for some time after that, sitting in the dark listening to slow jams and love songs. One night, when I knew I had it bad, the song "Shining Star" by the Manhattans came on the radio;

"Honey you, are my shining star, don't you go away."

Indeed, my shining star had gone, "with Fred," and I had never felt pain like that before. I was angry with Fred for a long time after that but we eventually made up, and Louise dumped him too, for a star football player. Yes!

Could it be that God's heart feels that kind of pain when we chase after other gods and ditch Him for "Fred"? Imagine Israel (God's shining star) talking with God for hours on the porch of the Tabernacle, or under the brightly lit moon and stars in the desert, how they would discuss His law, and how much the LORD loves them, and how much they loved God. How He looked intimately in their eyes while they huddled around the campfire; how He rescued them from the oppressive hand of Pharaoh by miracles and wonders. He promised to take care of them with a pillar of cloud by day and a pillar of fire by night to keep them warm. He fed them and protected them from foreign enemies, and would soon give them the pearl of the world, a land flowing with milk and honey. Yes, He is a jealous God, and to see Israel chase after other gods when He gave them His heart must have been cruel.

Listen to what the LORD says to Israel in (Jeremiah 2:25-33)

25 Do not run until your feet are bare
and your throat is dry.
But you said, 'It's no use!
I love foreign gods,
and I must go after them.'
26 "As a thief is disgraced when he is caught,
so the people of Israel are disgraced—
they, their kings and their officials,
their priests and their prophets.
27 They say to wood, 'You are my father,'
and to stone, 'You gave me birth.'
They have turned their backs to Me
and not their faces;
yet when they are in trouble, they say,
'Come and save us!'
28 Where then are the gods you made for yourselves?
Let them come if they can save you
when you are in trouble!
For you, Judah, have as many gods
as you have towns.
29 "Why do you bring charges against Me?
You have all rebelled against Me,"
declares the Lord.

30 "In vain I punished your people;
they did not respond to correction.
Your sword has devoured your prophets
like a ravenous lion.
31 "You of this generation, consider the word of the Lord:

"Have I been a desert to Israel

or a land of great darkness?
Why do My people say, 'We are free to roam;
we will come to You no more'?
32 Does a young woman forget her jewelry,
a bride her wedding ornaments?
Yet My people have forgotten me,
days without number.
33 How skilled you are at pursuing love!
Even the worst of women can learn from your ways.

Wow! Can't you feel the hurt God has for His people?

The god of wealth and prosperity; the god of career, fame, and fortune; the god of false love and false religion have taken His place. After all the time He has invested His love in "us" and spent every quarter in His pocket, to be with us, and we decide to date Fred, who doesn't even live in the same town. I think God does experience that kind of hurt, or else, how could we?

I believe this is why God sent a second Adam, not only because He loved us with all of His heart but to mend His broken heart. I believe God felt betrayed when Adam and Eve disobeyed Him even though He knew they would. His Son on the Cross is evident in how He felt. Jesus came not only to die for our sin and to restore a relationship between God and man but also, to show the world how painful our sin is to God. Every slap on the face of Christ, every spit, every lie told on Him, every untrue accusation, every betrayal, and denial of Him, every thorn pushed into His head, every piece of flesh ripped from His back by the whips, every nail in His hand and feet, the spear in His side and the nakedness of His body hanging on a cross, for all to see and mock as they passed by. God was letting us know how much all of mankind hurt Him? Jesus on the cross is how God feels about our loving other gods instead of Him. His first commandment, *"Thou shalt have no other gods before me,"* really means, thou shalt not bring any other god before My presence.

He displayed His hurt and His love that day Jesus hung on the cross. His unconditional love. A Godly love, an agape love, a love despite our disobedience and hatred toward Him. God, out of His massive, immense unquenchable love for you and me, painted the ultimate picture of love on the cross. ***He loved us as He loves Himself.*** The blood that dripped from His wounds was unlike the blood that was contaminated by sin in Adam. Jesus's blood was white as snow, red by nature, but white with righteousness and off-limits to the grips of sin. This was His free will: although He was tempted in every way He chose to obey God in every way, and therefore, His blood was pure enough, righteous enough, holy enough, perfect enough to cleans all those that would exchange their blood for His.

Think about it, as the Son of God He never had to have a free will, He was One with the Father, there was no need for "free will", only the will of the Godhead. However, when He became Jesus, God incarnate, the God/Man; The Son for the first time must choose to obey or disobey. This is why He is worthy of our praise and worthy of our worship and worthy of our obedience because He freely gave His very life for us when we didn't want it. In fact, we reviled it, and we treated Him worse than we treat each other. I was lost, He found me; I was blind, and He gave me sight; I was a prostitute, and He married me anyway.

We all have fallen short, we all have sinned, and we all need a Savior. Solomon said in Ecclesiastes, *"Let us hear the conclusion of the whole matter," this is our conclusion*:

"Fear God and keep His commandments, for this is men's all. For God will bring every work into judgment, including every secret thing, Whether good or evil."

Will you make Him your Savior today? Will you let Jesus teach you what it means to Love, to fill you with a love that conquers all; all hurt, all pain, all neglect, all unforgiveness and all bitterness toward your spouse? Let your work before Him, when you meet Him on the other side, be the work of Love.

Through the writing of this book, I have found my life's love, my wife Faith. We all share in common this thing called life. No one is perfect, we all make mistakes. God has set a plan for our life to do us good not evil. That means, His plan for my marriage and yours is good not evil. He will not allow the gates of hell to prevail against His ultimate plan for marriage and ministry.

To some degree, it's like Jesus's marriage to the church. We, His bride, argue with Him, fuss and fight with Him, don't want to submit to Him, or love Him sacrificially. The difference is Jesus is the perfect Husband; I am not. However, He has left me and you an instruction book that shares His secrets on how to become the perfect bride and husband and have a healthy and balanced marriage. In His Word, He is teaching me to love my wife as my own body; "Like a Butterfly with sore feet."

PRAYER

FATHER, thank You. Thank You for giving me the courage to be honest with myself and to expose my faults before the world to see. I thank You that through the writing of this book I found the man, husband, father and pastor you created me to be. It has not been easy admitting my sin, it has not been comfortable setting aside my pride, and it has not been effortless surrendering to Your will; but in it, healing has occurred, deliverance has taken place, a new found peace has settle upon me, and I now know that You are in the midst of all our circumstances. All my trials have shaped me, all my tribulations have grown me, all my pain has prepared me, and I can see how it is all working out for our good. I pray this book will encourage all those who read it to fight through the temptation to give up; I pray each one draws closer to Your Son Jesus, by the undertaking of being transformed by the renewing of their mind and quickening of their spirit. I pray we relentlessly seek the Holy Spirit to lead us and guide us in every aspect of our life. Father, I pray, husbands and wives set down their hurt, pride, and rigid posture toward one another and seek the greatest good in one another. I pray marriages be reconciled by the strength of Your grace, and the washing of Your word, and a true love for one another is forged during the darkest times.

I pray my wife and I come to that place in our marriage that is well pleasing in Your sight. I pray over my wife with the authority you have given me as her husband, I pray all her desires as a woman, mother and wife be fulfilled; for You said You will give us the desires of our heart. I pray for peace and prosperity even as her soul prospers, I pray she continues in becoming the mighty woman of God You have created her to be, a powerful force in your kingdom and to exemplify a Christ-like love to all those around her. I pray for protection over her and my daughters, I call the host of heaven to cover them with every arsenal needed to ward off the dark forces of the evil one. I pray Your face shines upon them and by the countenance of your presence surround them with Your love, grace, and mercy through Jesus Christ. Amen!

Words of Affirmation

A Balanced Life Through Habits of Success

In order to have a balanced life, you must develop good habits.

In His book [40]*The Greatest Salesman in The World*, Og Mandino writes of a young man "Hafid" desire to be the best salesman in the world. His boss, "Pathros," currently holds this title, but he is old. This greatest salesman has attained great wealth through the secrets of ten scrolls given him by his predecessor, however, the scrolls can only be given to those that are proven worthy, not by skill, but by an upright heart. These scrolls turn out to be secret habits worth more than any treasure. Most people think there is some kind of secret or wishing or skill needed to have balance and success. I have found, habits are what forms and shapes our present and future. I take some of these habits from his book and reword to fit my life, they are powerful, and many are scriptural; and I believe they can change your situation if you adhere to them faithfully. I would recommend you write them to fit your condition, then, the scroll must be read individually for thirty days straight;

[40] Og Mandino, *The Greatest Salesman in The World*, Bantam books published March 1974, pages 51-102

you cannot move to the next habit until you have completed the first. I have only applied six to my list.

We start with a pledge!

Today I begin a new thought and a new life. Today, I shed my old skin, which has too long suffered the bruises of failure and the wounds of mediocrity. Today, I was born anew and my birthplace is a vineyard where there is a fruit, the fruit of the Holy Spirit. Today I will pluck grapes of wisdom from the tallest and fullest vines in the vineyard of God's word. I will seek knowledge from the tree permitted, not the one forbidden. These were planted by God Himself and the wisest of men who have come before me, generation upon generation has used this knowledge and wisdom to guide them in all aspects of life. Today I will savor the taste of grapes from these vines, and assuredly I will swallow the seed of God's Spirit, and new life will sprout within me. The choices I have chosen are laden with opportunity, yet it is fraught with heartbreak and despair, I will gain the upper hand of doubt and immobilization. I will not fail, like others, for in my hands I now hold charts of hope, which will guide me through perilous waters to shores which only yesterday seemed but a dream.

Failure no longer will be my payment for struggle. Just as nature made no provisions for my body to tolerate pain, neither has it made any provision for my life to suffer failure. Failure, like pain, is alien to my life. In the past, I accepted it as I accepted pain. Now I reject it and I am prepared for wisdom and principles which will guide me out of the shadows into the sunlight of health, wealth, position, and happiness far beyond my most extravagant dreams. For He has come to give me life, and it, more abundantly. Failure is always described but one way. Failure is man's inability to reach his goals in life, whatever they may be. In truth, the only difference between those who have failed and those who have succeeded lies in their habits of hope in God. Good habits are the keys to all success. Bad habits are the unlocked door to failure. First, form good habits of belief in God's word and become their slave. I will read God's word daily. "For when an act becomes easy through consistent repetition, it becomes a pleasure to perform, and if it is a pleasure to perform it, then it is in man's nature to perform it often. As the words of scripture are consumed by my mysterious mind "soul," I will begin to awake each morning, with a vitality I have never known before. My vigor will increase, my enthusiasm will rise, my desire to meet the world will overcome every fear I once knew at sunrise, and I will be happier than I ever believed it possible to be even in my trials, tribulations, and afflictions, for they will no longer work against me, but for me.

One: The Habit to Love

The first habit I attend to is, Love. Love is our greatest weapon; it conquers all. I will master this art, and soon, all must bow to it. My wife, the church, and people will question my reasoning; my words they may distrust; my motives may be suspicious, but my true, sincere love will warm all hearts just as the sun warms the ocean waters that reach the beach.

I will greet each day with a purpose to love. To love God, my wife, the church, and my neighbor and life itself. I will learn to endure the struggles and sufferings of this world with love. I will overcome the attraction to retaliate when I feel disrespected, insulted, and treated unfairly; I will not fight evil with evil but with love.

I will fixate my mind to love my enemies who will become my friends, and with love, they will become my brothers; I will begin to see the glass half full in my wife, not the glass half empty; I will find a reason to applaud my detractors for the remaining light they do have in their soul, and this love will sway them from critics to supporters. When I am tempted to lose it, criticize or complain, I will find the voice of love instead or remain a mute until I can find the words of love. I will rejoice for those that have helped me, for they have inspired me, and I will expose my love even to those that hate me, for it will empower me. I will love them, and there is nothing they can do about it. I will not intentionally say "I love you to my enemy," but internally through my non-aggressive posture, eyes of light, the smile on my face, and the warmth of my presence; this will soon deflate their motives, for their guilt will be as coals of fire on their heads.

And lastly, but more importantly, I will love myself. I will not allow my heart to be bitter or contain un-forgiveness for past sins against me or sins I have committed against others. I will overcome the scar of painful memories with the exhilaration of love. I will forgive myself, for my Father in heaven has forgiven me first for eternity; I will love myself, for my Father in heaven has commanded His Love toward me. Yes, love will be my motto. It will be my habit! "For if I have no other qualities, I can succeed with love alone."

Two: The Habit of Persistence

Love is the foundation, but persistence is the method for success. When a home is being built, it must be built on a strong foundation, but without the persistence to erect the frame or run the wiring and plumbing through its walls, without the correct angle of the roof to keep the rain from gathering in one place, the house will not be livable. Love is the base, but I must have the persistence to build the rest of the house, I must have persistence to succeed. To build a stable and balanced marriage, ministry, or business, I will be tenacious and not whimsical. Jesus says *"No one who puts his hand to the plow and looks back is not fit for the kingdom of God."* (Luke 9:62) ESV

Og Mandino writes, "In the Orient young bulls are tested for the fight arena in a certain manner. Each is brought to the ring and allowed to attack a picador who pricks them with a lance. The bravery of each bull is then rated with care according to the number of times he demonstrates his willingness to charge in spite of the sting of the blade. Henceforth will I recognize that each day I am tested by life and like manner. If I persist, if I continue to try, if I continue to charge forward, I will succeed. I will persist until I succeed, despite the sting of the blade."

"I can do all things through Christ who gives me strength." (Philippians 4:13)

"And let us not grow weary of doing good, for in due season we will reap, if we do not give up" (Galatians 6:9) ESV

I was never created for defeat, and I was reborn with victory already before me. I cannot lose, I cannot fail, if I persist in faith. I am endowed with unbelievable immense power when I know the war is already won. Winning the battle makes me stronger and the suffering gives me more anointing and the affliction improve my character. I will win, no matter how low the valley or how dark the cloud, how thick the forest, how deep the waters, I will succeed, succeed in my marriage, in my ministry, in my church, on my job. Whatever the battle, I know that victory is mine.

I will press toward my goal every day, always will I take another step despite what yesterday's steps may or may not have acquired; even though some steps may bring failure, the next step might bring success, for who knows if the next corner is filled will all my expectations. "Never, never, never give up!" My steps can lead down or up, it depends on where I want to go.

I must remove words of doubt, for they are seeds for failure. In my marriage, we have never uttered the words to divorce; I forbid it to slip past my mouth; I might have thought it, but I soon replaced it with, Never, never, never give up! Faint not in doing good, and we shall reap a God-pleasing marriage.

I will try and try again until I learn to love my wife as Christ loves the church. I will try and try again to walk worthy of my calling until I hear the words, "Well done my good and faithful servant." I will try and try again until I learn how to bring my body and mouth under subjection until my sin is conquered. As long as I have breath in me, I will succeed, I will persist, for I know God is faithful, and my labor is not in vain.

Three: The Habit of Correct Self-Image

I was created in the image of God! Let that sink in for just a moment.

I am how God sees Himself when He looks at me, He sees Himself. These are not arrogant words, or words of pride, these are my Creators words. These are the character traits He instilled in me. I am His glory! Again, let that sink in....

I was created to reflect all the goodness of God, the greatness of God, the beauty of God, the power of God, the love, grace, and mercy of God. I am not concerned how others see me, for if I know who I reflect; they will see the source of my reflection; and if others chose to be blinded to this radiant glory, it's not because of the light within me, it's because either I have not let it shine, or they prefer darkness. In addition to that, there is no one else like me; I am unique. Never again will there be another as I am. No one can preach like me, teach like me, sing like me, sell like me, cook, write, or think like me. Nothing in all of creation can meet the likeness of me, and yet, I strive to become more like my Creator. I will not attempt to be as someone else, only what God has created me to be, which is sufficient. Likewise, I will see others in their uniqueness and appreciate their differences and applaud their similarities. Although I am unique and created in His image, I will keep a humble spirit and pull others to strive for all that God has for their life. I will be His glory!

I will no longer be satisfied with mediocrity or averageness. I can accomplish far more than I have, and I will, for my Savior, said I will do greater things than He. I have a purpose on this earth, and in this life, I forbid the enemy to cloud my mind with anything else. I will increase my knowledge of who I am and whose I am through God's word. Scripture will be as an ornament around my neck; I will search for it more than rubies or pearls, more than gold or silver, even more than the treasures of Solomon. It will be my habit day and night to read the book my Creator has given me, to show me "me" as He shows me Himself in His word and through His Son.

Four: The Habit of Living for Today

"So do not worry about tomorrow; for tomorrow will worry about itself. Each day has enough trouble of its own." (Matthew 6:34) AMP

Worry is the instrument of Satan. Worry can paralyze you into doing nothing; it produces unnecessary fear; it prompts a premature action for something that may never happen. I must live each day for today, leave yesterday where it belongs; let tomorrow come on its own merits. Plan, yes, but be pliable, for tomorrow has her own plans for me. Why should I waste energy on what has already happened, yesterday's disappointment, failures, and misfortunes? Why use up brain cells chasing after *what if's*? Can I recant all my mistakes from yesterday, no? Then I will no longer think of them anymore. I will forget those things which are behind; I will sail them as cargo on the ship of chalked-up experience. I will not be muzzled by yesterday's displeasures, nor will I be robbed of today's glory or troubled with tomorrow's escapades. Can I place tomorrow's gold into today's purse? Can I reach back into yesterday and grab the treasure I lost? No! I will be grateful and thankful for today, for this could be my last.

None of us are promised tomorrow, we are here today and gone tomorrow like chaff in the wind. So, I will not take for granted the blessings as well as the challenges of today, for all things are working for my good. I will not let the beauty of my wife's eyes go unnoticed, or her draw-dropping dimples, or her perfect smile, or her curvaceous body. I will not overlook her inner beauty of empathy and compassion, or her dedication to our family, and the work ethic she bestows. I will hug my children more than yesterday, talk with them with more words and listen with bigger ears.

I will be even more thankful today than yesterday and more so tomorrow than today, for God has blessed me with more than I could imagine and deserve. Even in my distresses, I am blessed because it could have been worse. I will no longer allow Satan to cause me to focus on what's wrong with my life, or marriage, or career, health, or ministry, but what's right about them. I will see the good today until it overshadows the bad from yesterday. What will a man lose today, searching for the whole world tomorrow? What dying man can purchase another breath though he will give all he has? No, my friend, for this is the day that the Lord has made, let me rejoice and be glad in it; today, today, today!

Five: The Habit of Controlled Emotions

"Weak is he who permits his thoughts to control his actions; strong is he who forces his actions to control his thoughts."

"Better a patient person than a warrior, one with self-control than one who takes a city." (Proverbs 16:32) NIV

"But the fruit of the Spirit is love, joy, peace, forbearance, kindness, goodness, faithfulness, gentleness, and self-control. Against such things, there is no law." (Galatians 5:22, 23) NIV

Usually, I can control my emotions. However, one adversary of mine is anger. It can rise up in me without warning. I can feel when it starts to simmer within, and if not measured, the floodgates of emotions can erupt like a volcano. Generally, I can catch it before it does minor damage, but there is a rare point of no return, and that place scares me. I am told I inherited it from my father, it seems most of my siblings have the same issue. Righteous anger is not a sin. Jesus often became angry, but His indignation is always honest and just, mine is not. Since becoming a pastor, I have learned to temper my impatience but the lava right below the mountain is always waiting to rise.

However, today, I will be master of my emotions. I will no longer be a victim of the seed of my father but be victorious from the seed of my FATHER in heaven. I will become more familiar with this emotion that causes me to act out of my Creator's character. I will learn its formula and rewrite it to benefit me and not to have charge over me. I will not let outside circumstances dictate the thermostat of my emotions, nor will I succumb to the inner voice of vindication. I must never relinquish control but be power under control.

When sadness comes, I will not be unapproachable; when despair and doubt creep in, I will not become frantic; when hurt and shame take up residence in my heart, they will be evicted; when jealousy and envy lead me to gossip, I will not have a forked tongue but words of honey. I will be master of my emotions. Anger is an emotion from God, it is not bad until we do bad things while under its influence. If anger comes from injustice, it's a good emotion. If anger comes because I give up, it can work in my favor by way of motivation. I will be master of my emotions. I will understand my emotions but also the emotions of my brother. I will study his emotions, for if he is not in control, my controlled emotions can guide his.

Six: The Habit of Assimilation

No environment is beyond my reach, I am the master of my environment, it cannot control me, it cannot contain me, it cannot persuade my present or my future. Everywhere my feet tread will be my domain, I was created to have dominion. Authority and power are my companions, they go before me, bulldozing fear and indecisiveness clearing a successful path. I am able to adapt, adjust, and integrate into any environment and bend it to my will, to my purpose. I am the element of change. I am the cause of inspiration in the midst of desperation. I am the light that shines in the dark and my Creator has designed me for this very purpose: *"I shall become all things to all people, that I might win some."* I will make every situation better, not worse.

As a man bends a spoon, I will bend undesirable places, people, and perceptions to my will, for I have the authority from my Father to do so. He has given me this power, this treasure within my earthen vessel. What is this treasure? It is the light of the gospel, and I will let it shine to transform darkness into light; and if my light is hidden, it is hidden to those that are blinded. Blinded by mediocrity, laziness, status quo, averageness, ordinaries, and lack of ambition. However, even then, if given enough time, this glorious light can enlighten them to their blindness, and they too will become masters of their environment.

This is my purpose, not just wealth and power, but eternal purpose. A purpose, a treasure laid up in heaven, where moths nor rust can destroy it, and thieves can steal. Because of the strength my Father gives me, I will bear with the scruples of the weak, and help him to become strong; I will edify him and motivate him until he does.

This is my duty; it is not arrogance, or pompous self-promotion, for I am strong only by the grace of God. I am only strong because He is in me and I in Him. Without Him, I am nothing and can do nothing, I am weak but I am also strong because I have turned over my weakness to Him, who is far stronger than I.

Today, I will become a valuable friend to the weak, to the blind. How will I do this? Through actions, not words, I will become my words; I will put my words into action. When my brother is sad, I will be sad with him; when he is joyous, I will rejoice with him; when he is in the midst of the trial, I will be in the midst with him. I will become accountable to him; he will count on me, and I will not let him down. We will change the environment together; we will adapt to the mood of the circumstance. I will throw away the rigidity of pride and un-compromised and inflexibility. In this, my value will grow, my worth will be sought, my character will be desired because it is the character of Christ. This character will go beyond my brother, my church, my family; it will find its way in the workplace, the Home Owners Association board, the Neighborhood committee, the school, the halls of community service. I will affect and infect every place my feet tread upon. I will fit in to make one comfortable, but I will also stand out to help them see their error; in this is a true value, sincere love, and needed sacrifice that makes an impression far beyond that moment. Though they might be offended at first, they will soon realize the truth of the matter, and they will be set free from their offense.

I can multiply my value some 30, some 60, some 100-fold; the more my value, the more I must sacrifice. Little value, little sacrifice, exceeding value, exceeding sacrifice. To whom much is given, much is expected. I will become less to become more, I will serve, not to be served. I will seek the lesser seat, not the head of the table and with sincere humility be exalted. The longer wine is agitated through the process of fermentation the more valuable it is. There will be agitation before value. Diamonds are first coal pushed and pressured through the earth by volcanic eruptions, but it has no real value until it has been cut; the better the cut the more valuable it is.

To be master of my environment, I must be able to endure the pressure and heat of that environment, and then let the experience of that pressure cut away things that make me less valuable. Therefore, the sacrifice is ***worth*** it. I am a master of my environment.

I will do the work others will not, I will go the extra mile not required, I will give my shirt and my coat and not expect it to be returned, I will always reach for a higher goal once a goal is met, I will not be satisfied with yesterday's success, but look for a new hill to conquer today. These are my inner desires, I will write the vision on the wall to make it plain, but I will not boast when they are achieved; once achieved, I will write another vision and let the accomplishment boast rather than my tongue, only in my suffering for Christ will I boast.

These are my habits, to say them and believe them each day, and soon what has been said, and what has been believed, will come to past and bring a balanced life.

About the Author

Pastor Eric L Jordan has preached the Word of God for over twenty years. He is the Founder and Senior Pastor of A Breath of Praise Community Church for over a decade. He and his wife, Faith, have been married for thirty-one years, have three daughters, and live in Round Rock, Texas.

Like a Butterfly with Sore Feet, he gives a candid and personal account of the struggles of assessing the cost of an unbalanced Marriage, Family, and Ministry. Through his journey of trials and wanting to give up, you will find the courage to overcome the temptation to throw in the towel, the strength to defeat the dark forces against you, and a restored love for your spouse. In his flaws as a husband, father, and pastor, you will learn how to overcome your weaknesses and draw on a faith that is available to all of us, a faith that will bring down spiritual strongholds in your marriage and ministry and bring peace and balance to your life.

His passion is to help restore broken marriages, encourage perseverance and determination in difficult times of ministry. He inspires people to walk in the God-given authority created within them, and remind us, "all things" work for the good, to those that love God and called according to His purpose, even in our most trying periods. He teaches us how to turn the enemy's weapons against him so that *no weapon* formed against you will prosper.